224 Remedial Ideas

Also of Interest

Yes, They Can!
Kenneth Weber

224 Remedial Ideas

W. C. Nesbit
Memorial University of Newfoundland

N. H. Hadley
Memorial University of Newfoundland

M. L. Marshall
Mary Queen of Peace School
St. John's, Newfoundland

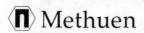 Methuen

Toronto   New York   London   Sydney   Wellington

Canadian Cataloguing in Publication Data

Nesbit, Wayne C., 1943-
  224 remedial ideas

ISBN 0-458-93760-6

1. Remedial teaching—Handbooks, manuals, etc.
2. Learning disabilities. I. Hadley, Norman H., 1944-   II. Marshall, Mary L., 1953-
III. Title.

LB1029.R4N48   371.9   C78-001569-X

Printed and bound in Canada

1 2 3 4 5   79 80 81 82

Contents

Foreword

The purpose of this handbook is twofold: (1) to provide a brief descriptive introduction to specific types of learning problems; and (2) to present a number of noncommercial remedial suggestions in a convenient and practical form.

1/Gross Motor Movement

When we speak of gross motor activities and gross motor development, we are focussing upon movement and development with large body muscles. It is the usual case that gross motor development precedes fine motor development. That is, the child learns to control movements involving the entire musculature prior to the acquisition of control of wrists, fingers, toes.

The proximodistal principle describes the developmental tendency to acquire control of the large muscle groups toward the centre of the body before acquiring control of parts lying at the body's extremities. The cephalocaudal principle, a parallel developmental principle, is utilized to describe the developmental tendency for motor control to move in a head to "tail" direction. These principles have been verified by numerous researchers who have established general developmental age trends based upon studies involving hundreds of children.

At birth the neonate has a very limited awareness of his surroundings, and it is only as the first months pass that he begins to make even a gross differentiation between his body and that of his mother. It is often a part of the mother such as her hands or her breast that is recognized first as external to himself. His awareness of his own body is equally undifferentiated and he reacts to physical discomfort in an organismic fashion. At first his movements are involuntary and his response to a stimulus such as a bottle, a toy or a face involves the entire body—head, arms and legs move in an uncontrolled fashion.

By the age of twelve to fourteen months most children have achieved locomotion and are far along the way to adequate gross motor control. During childhood these movements become more refined and complex. For the child who demonstrates a lag in motor development or lack of motor control, educational problems related to fine motor coordination, body concept, directionality and eye-hand coordination are somewhat predictable.

A number of researchers have attempted to relate a lack of motor control to problems in the acquisition of reading and language skills. It is the authors' view that motor training will not teach a child to read or improve specific problems such as auditory discrimination as some writers would lead one to believe. Nevertheless, adequate motor development fosters self-confidence and encourages a child as he confronts problems related to academic skills.

Studies of the relationship of motor to academic development are currently in progress and more emphasis is being placed on proper physical education programming. One program which incorporates the idea of adequate motor development is the *Battle Creek Physical Education Program* developed by A. Van Holst of London, Ontario. This program is being explored in a number of St. John's, Newfoundland schools and has been reported to be worthwhile in that it provides a general physical education program and, at the same time, can be geared to the specific weaknesses of individual children.

The most accurate method to assess a child's motor development is in terms of an established scale which outlines age guidelines from birth onward. Various scales have been developed but these are not always available to the classroom teacher. One method which provides a somewhat less precise measure than a standardized scale is teacher observation. Granted, there are limitations; but the teacher can screen for problems related to motor development by carefully observing her students during regular classroom activities. If a student's general motor control appears to be inferior to his chronological age-mates, there may be reason to observe more carefully to discover areas which are most problematic. There are a number of symptoms of impaired or delayed motor development. The teacher should take note of motor patterns such as the following:

1. Cannot skip or hop properly;
2. Difficulty balancing on one foot or walking a straight line;
3. Problems copying another person's movements;
4. Irregular gait while walking or running;
5. Trouble with tying and buttoning;
6. Inability to kick, catch or throw a ball or bean bag;
7. Bumps into and trips over objects which are large and visible;
8. Frequently drops things.

When a child's motor performance includes a number of these motor patterns, the teacher is warranted to conclude that the child has a gross motor problem. The source of the problem may range from a developmental lag to minimal brain dysfunction. The teacher is not in a position to comment upon etiology and should not attempt to present the problem to parents or others in a context other than observational. "I have noted that John has difficulty when asked to hop, throw the ball or walk a straight line," represents the type of observational data which provides a basis for remedial programming.

A good gross motor program includes the following aims:

1. To achieve adequate body balance;
2. To gain control over the movement of large body muscles;
3. To refine the large muscle activity into unified flowing patterns;
4. To build self-confidence through improved motor performance.

Essentials of a motor program which centres upon such aims are presented.

Suggested Strategies

Rolling: the ability to turn the body in a controlled manner while lying in a prone position.

Remedial Objective: to teach the children awareness of basic body movement.

Prescriptive teaching strategy 1:

Direct the child to lie on his back with his arms flat on the floor over his head. Instruct him to roll over on his stomach, rolling first to the right and then to the left. At first, this exercise is done with the child's eyes open. Then it is repeated with the eyes closed.

Prescriptive teaching strategy 2:

Ask the child to roll over a number of times to the right and then to the left. A variation is to ask the child to hold an object in his hands while he is rolling in response to the teacher's directions.

Prescriptive teaching strategy 3:

Variations on strategy 2 include: (a) rolling with one hand over the head and the other hand by the side; (b) rolling with feet together and both arms at the sides; (c) rolling with feet together and arms crossed over the chest; (d) rolling up and down grassy inclines.

Prescriptive teaching strategy 4:

This exercise should be performed on a mat or a rug. Tell the child to crouch with his knees bent and his hands placed flat on the floor by his sides. When his head touches the floor he pushes his body forward with his feet until he rolls over and lands on his back.

Crawling: the ability to draw the body along the floor using the hands and knees.

Remedial Objective: to begin coordination of the movement of the upper and lower limbs in a cross-lateral fashion.

Prescriptive teaching strategy 5:

Once the child has learned to crawl, the teacher directs the child to crawl quickly like a spider, crawl slowly like a snail, crawl like a snake.

Prescriptive teaching strategy 6:

The child tries different ways of crawling including the following: (a) using the right arm and left leg and then left arm and right leg; (b) using left side limbs together and then right side limbs together; (c) crawling using the arms only. Observe that in (c) the child's stomach touches the floor with the arms as the means of movement.

Prescriptive teaching strategy 7:

Instruct the child to crawl toward a goal. Mark paths on the floor and have a number of children begin at the same time. The first child to reach the goal wins a prize placed at the end of the path.

Prescriptive teaching strategy 8:

The children crawl an obstacle course which includes crawling through, over, under and around objects. For example, the child crawls through the legs of a chair, over a small box, under a table, around a table and finally through an open-ended box.

Sitting: the ability to maintain balance and posture in a semi-upright position.

Remedial Objective: to teach children how to acquire and maintain appropriate posture.

Prescriptive teaching strategy 9:

The child sits up straight on a chair with both feet flat on the floor. He folds his hands and counts to ten.

Prescriptive teaching strategy 10:

Ask the children to sit on the floor in various positions: (a) like a dog begging for food; (b) Indian-fashion with legs crossed and arms folded across the chest; (c) with knees on the floor and with buttocks resting on heels; (d) with legs extended straight in front.

Prescriptive teaching strategy 11:

The student sits upright in his desk and sees how long he can balance a book on his head. This activity could be made more difficult by placing other objects on the book.

Prescriptive teaching strategy 12:

Teach children how to relax while sitting at the desk while maintaining correct posture. The child sits all the way back in his chair with feet flat on the floor. His arm rests on his desk so that he can write comfortably.

Prescriptive teaching strategy 13:

Instruct the children to sit on chairs in a circle. They pick up a ball between their feet and pass it to their neighbour. The person who drops it has to leave the circle. The winner is the last one left sitting in the circle.

Walking: to move in a controlled manner.

Remedial Objective: to help children acquire balance and coordination in walking.

Prescriptive teaching strategy 14:

Walk forward lifting the feet on a marked path, sideways, tiptoe, each time having the arms held in a different position.

Prescriptive teaching strategy 15:

Direct the child to walk a line sideways without crossing one foot over the other. Have him start at one end of the line and return. Repeat with the child crossing one foot over the other.

Prescriptive teaching strategy 16:

Place boxes in a defined path. Every time the child takes a step, he has to place his foot in a box. If the child knows his left and right, the boxes could be marked to indicate which foot to use for each step.

Prescriptive teaching strategy 17:

With masking tape, mark out a ladder on the floor. The child has to walk forward and backward between the rungs. In addition, an actual ladder could be employed.

Prescriptive teaching strategy 18:

There are various animal walks that can be imitated. Show the children pictures of animals (i.e., elephants, roosters, kangaroos, ostriches and ducks) and have them try to walk the way these animals do.

Throwing: the ability to project an object with appropriate force and direction.

Remedial Objective: to teach accuracy and directionality in throwing.

Prescriptive teaching strategy 19:

The child is required to throw the ball to a catcher. Gradually the distance between the thrower and the catcher is increased. The size of the ball used would decrease when the child became competent with a particular size. Bean bags could also be used.

Prescriptive teaching strategy 20:

Take a large open-ended box and tape it to the wall. The child is required to throw a ball into the box. Box size could be varied.

Prescriptive teaching strategy 21:

Draw a circle on the floor and have the child throw a bean bag into it. He competes with himself, trying to improve on successive trials.

Prescriptive teaching strategy 22:

Mark out a series of lines beginning a few feet from the child and at increased distances. The child is instructed to throw a basketball to each mark in turn, beginning with the nearest mark.

Prescriptive teaching strategy 23:

The child is instructed to stand in a set position and to throw a ball to his left and to his right without moving the lower section of his body. Next he attempts to perform the throws with a target in mind, i.e., a bucket to the left.

Jumping: the ability to use the leg muscles in a coordinated manner to rise from the ground.

Remedial Objective: to teach children to improve their balance as well as muscular coordination.

Prescriptive teaching strategy 24:

Have the child jump first using both feet, then the right foot and finally the left foot. An extension of this activity would involve the use of a skipping rope.

Prescriptive teaching strategy 25:

The child jumps forward on both feet, then on his right foot and then on his left foot. As the child's jumping improves, low objects are introduced as obstacles to jump over.

Prescriptive teaching strategy 26:

Ask the child to jump forward with both feet wide apart and at the same time clap his hands over his head.

Prescriptive teaching strategy 27:

The children stand on a line and jump forward as far as possible from the standing position.

Prescriptive teaching strategy 28:

Use a ladder made of masking tape and instruct the child to jump forward and backward through the rungs. If available, a real ladder could be used.

Skipping: the ability to use the feet in a coordinated manner with or without the use of a skipping rope.

Remedial Objective: To improve body coordination and control in the lower limbs.

Prescriptive teaching strategy 29:

The child moves his arms in a circular motion while going through the motions of skipping, hopping first forward and then backward. The exercise can be repeated with the child hopping on one foot and then the other.

Prescriptive teaching strategy 30:

With a skipping rope, have the child repeat strategy 29 using both feet at first and then alternating feet.

Prescriptive teaching strategy 31:

With a skipping rope, have the child skip forward around the room. With more children participating, a game could be organized with the winner being the first one to reach a finish point.

Prescriptive teaching strategy 32:

With two children holding the ends of a long skipping rope, a third child skips forward then backward.

2 / Body Image

Body image requires consideration of four major questions: "What are the [body] parts? What can they do? How do you make them do it? What space do they occupy while doing it?" (Channey and Kephart, 1968).

The term body image refers to the variety of ways in which the child understands his own body, its movement and its uses. Stevens (1971) postulates that there are three levels of competence in developing the body image:

A. Identification of body parts and planes;
B. Relationship between body and objects;
C. Movement of the body in and through space.

Progression in terms of competence at these levels should be from A to B to C. This means that a child who has not mastered A level skills could possibly experience difficulty in moving the body in and through space.

A child who is unable to name the body part pointed to by the teacher or is unable to point to tricky parts involving awareness of body planes, such as "front of nose," "back of knees," "side of nose," possibly reveals problems in identifying body parts and planes. A child who repeatedly makes errors in locating an object held in various positions around him in relation to his body—e.g., behind his back, in front of his nose, etc.—would demonstrate problems in the relationship between body and objects. These problems are also indicated when a child has difficulty with performance tasks requiring him to touch various parts of his body to selected objects; e.g., touching his back to the wall. Children showing problems in moving the body in and through space will lack awareness that they have six main directions: up and down space, front and back space, left and right space. Efficient movement depends on awareness of these directions in relation both to one's own body and to general physical space. These problems may also be shown by frequent errors in answers to questions such as:

Can you put your hands behind you?

Can you put your chest (front) behind you?

What is the bottom of your space (i.e., seat if he is sitting, knees if he is kneeling, or feet if he is standing)?

In addition, frequent errors in performance when asked to stand at the teacher's right, to crawl backwards toward the front of the room, or to put his feet above his head may suggest a lack of awareness in moving the body in and through space.

Since much of our learning is based on directionality, it is important to learn to discriminate between right and left. Simple arithmetic processes such as addition and subtraction progress from right to left whereas equations are written from left to right. Preschool children may manifest great difficulty in discriminating between visual stimuli that differ only in orientation,—e.g., *b*, *d*, *p* and *q*. The child will generally learn to differentiate between up and down based on the direction of the stem (*b* and *p*) before he differentiates between right and left (*p* and *q* as well as *b* and *d*). Some children, however, lag behind in this development and continue with letter reversals (Ross, 1976).

If a child has problems in reversals, a thorough assessment should be made of his competence in identifying body parts and planes and in relating his body to environmental objects. Several prominent researchers in learning disabilities have even suggested that improvement in body image is accompanied by improvement in certain problems related to reading such as reversals.

The teacher should also note difficulties in activities in which the child:

1. Selects too small or too large a space for activities which require movement of various parts of the body;
2. Is unable to move one member of a pair of limbs without moving the other (unable to move one arm without moving the other);
3. Is unable to move one limb on one side of the body and a different limb on the other side (moving the left leg and the right arm simultaneously);
4. Is unable to effectively utilize the kinesthetic feedback from the movement itself but must visually monitor the movement and position of his limbs. Many children and even adults when learning to dance must constantly "look at their feet" to ascertain their location and "what they are doing";
5. Unable to locate *left* or *right* in persons or objects outside himself. Although the child may be able to point to his own "left foot" or "right hand" (laterality), he may have considerable trouble in locating your "left foot" or "right hand" (directionality).

If such difficulties persist, it may suggest problems in the area of body image and it will be necessary to implement remediation.

Since the introduction of the body image concept into Special Education, four major methods have been favoured to measure the integrity of body image in children:

1. The drawing of the human figure: distortion of details, omission of parts, variations in size and differences in emphasis have been the criteria for inferring confusion in the image the drawer held of his own body. According to Morris and Whiting (1971) there are difficulties with this kind of "projective test" in that the product may represent in addition to the body concept itself:
   (a) The drawing ability of the child;
   (b) A projection of the idealized self-image;
   (c) An expression of his concept of others;
   (d) The influence of cultural factors;
   (e) Aspects of the broader self-concept including personality attributes.
2. Labelling of body parts by written or spoken responses.
3. Requiring the child to watch a movement sequence and the teacher to then observe the child's problems in performing and describing the movement activity (Stone, 1968; Jones, 1970).
4. Having the child look at a list of words with an equal number of body and non-body words positioned in random order. After one minute the list is removed and the child is asked to write down as many words as he can remember. The scoring method in this instance is to total the "body" words and to subtract the "non-body" words (Fisher, 1964). Although short-term memory is involved in the recall of the words, the assumption appears to be that the child's familiarity with either body or non-body words will influence his recall.

Suggested Strategies

Body localization: the ability to identify body parts.

Remedial Objective: to teach the child the parts of the body and their interaction.

Prescriptive teaching strategy 33:

The teacher points to a part of her body and asks the student to locate the part on his own body. As the child becomes competent in doing this, he can begin naming the various parts. Finally, the child is able to point out body parts.

Prescriptive teaching strategy 34:

The children pretend that they are toy soldiers. They have to follow directions. One child is designated to be the general and the others have to watch him and imitate his movements.

Prescriptive teaching strategy 35:

Show pictures with body parts missing. Have them identify the parts that are missing and fill them in.

Prescriptive teaching strategy 36:

Ask the child to estimate how many jumps he must take to reach a certain goal. Let him do the jumping and see how close he comes to his estimate.

Directionality: the ability to distinguish up from down, left from right, forward from back.

Remedial Objective: to teach awareness of directions in relationship to the body.

Prescriptive teaching strategy 37:

Instruct the child to close his eyes. A sound is made somewhere in the room and he is asked to identify whether the sound came from behind, in front, to the left or to the right. After he has responded, he opens his eyes and checks.

Prescriptive teaching strategy 38:

Direct the child to follow directions in drawing. For example, draw a sun in the *top left-hand* corner of the page, and pond at the *bottom* of the page, and two ducks in the *middle* of the pond.

Prescriptive teaching strategy 39:

Blindfold the child and direct him to identify various parts of the body which the teacher touches.

Prescriptive teaching strategy 40:

The children draw parts of the body and assemble them into a picture of the body.

Body spatial orientation: the ability to identify the position the body occupies in relation to its surroundings.

Remedial Objective: to increase awareness of efficient movement through space.

Prescriptive teaching strategy 41:

Create mazes within the classroom by moving furniture and ask the child to walk through them without bumping into any of the obstacles. Gradually reduce the distance between objects in the maze so that better body control is required.

Prescriptive teaching strategy 42:

Play "follow me" by having the children follow the teacher through an obstacle course. The concepts "over," "under," "in front of," "behind," "on" and "around" could be taught during this activity.

Prescriptive teaching strategy 43:

A full-length mirror can be beneficial in teaching the child to identify body parts and boundaries. The child imitates another person's actions while studying his own movements in the mirror.

Prescriptive teaching strategy 44:

The child follows simple directions in moving his body. These might include "stamp your left foot," "touch your right ear with your left hand," etc.

Prescriptive teaching strategy 45:

Present the child with a picture in which there is a central figure as well as several other figures. The child must tell where each figure is in relation to the central figure.

Balance: the ability to maintain or move the body efficiently in relation to gravitational planes.

Remedial Objective: to increase sensitivity to proprioceptive or internal body cues.

Prescriptive teaching strategy 46:

From a kneeling position the child grasps his feet with his hands so that his heels are as close as possible to his back. He remains kneeling in this position for fifteen to twenty seconds.

Prescriptive teaching strategy 47:

Walk a balance beam in a heel to toe progression. At first arms may be fully extended like an airplane. Later the activity is repeated with hands resting by the sides.

Prescriptive teaching strategy 48:

Many strategies can be incorporated into the use of the balance beam, for example, walking forward, backward, sideways, picking up objects on the beam and replacing them, hopping on right or left foot and carrying objects while walking.

Prescriptive teaching strategy 49:

Have the child balance a ruler on one foot. The child is required to raise his foot while balancing the ruler.

Prescriptive teaching strategy 50:

The child walks a prescribed course while balancing a book on his head. At the end of the course, he has to bend his knees and return in a crouched position.

3/ Fine Motor Coordination

Fine motor coordination describes the ability to control and coordinate the small muscles. It is often difficult to define this ability as distinct from other abilities associated with motor output. As an example, throwing involves gross motor ability to a certain extent but also involves fine motor coordination. Aiming depends upon finger movement while the strength for the throw comes from the larger muscles. Similarly, tracing and cutting involve eye-motor coordination and error demonstrated in performing such tasks may be caused by either the visual perceptual component or the fine motor component of the task. What is being said is that human behaviour cannot be neatly segmented; the sensorium functions in an integrated fashion. Therefore, many activities involve both large and small muscle groups.

With this consideration in mind, it is safe to say that some tasks have as their chief component fine motor coordination. Historically, problems related to gross motor development have been the concern of physical educators, while problems related to fine motor coordination have been referred to special educators and vocational therapists. While balance, ambulation and the movement of the body through space tend to relate more closely to the gross end of the motor continuum, tasks which require less space and less energy expenditure are defined as small muscle or fine motor tasks.

Eye-hand coordination, as mentioned previously, is a hybrid involving both ocular control and fine motor control. In a visual sense, eye-hand coordination involves the ability to maintain the eye in a relatively fixed position when necessary, to move the eye sequentially while following an object (the hand) and to study a series of objects by controlled movement. Eye-hand coordination is represented in the first of five subtests which comprise Frostig's Developmental Test of Visual Perception. The eye-motor coordination subtest consists of drawing uninterrupted lines between prescribed boundaries which become increasingly narrow with each successive item.

It is imperative that the child be able to match what he is doing visually with what he is doing motorically. The experiences must weld together in a meaningful way. Bortner (1968) has noted three stages in the development of perceptual-motor match: (1) control of single acts; (2) control of continuous activities; and (3) control of sequential acts. In most cases these stages follow each other in a developmental sequence.

In the course of human development, responses tend to become more and more differentiated. This occurs in terms of emotional, motor and mental output. The earlier organismic excitement predicated by the onset of a stimulus is replaced by an increasingly larger repertoire of differentiated behaviours. Early attempts at fine motor tasks characterized by lack of ability to juxtapose finger and thumb, and the simultaneous mimicking of hand manipulation by the hand not involved in the task, are replaced by more coordinated movements and the establishment of a dominant or preferred hand.

The most problematic aspect of school experience for the child with poor fine motor skills is the frustration and consequent decrement in self-esteem associated with not being able to perform adequately. Considering the sizeable segment of primary and elementary curricula which is devoted to printing, colouring and cutting, we can conclude that the child who has a marked problem with small muscle control is regularly frustrated. Attempting to form geometric shapes and space evenly between the lines on a page can be anxiety ridden.

A list of symptoms of small muscle control problems is presented. Once again it is necessary to emphatically state that the child's behaviour must be considered in a developmental context. If a five-year-old has difficulty colouring within boundaries, it indicates nothing. If all the children at seven years can print within the lines and one child cannot, then there is cause to question (not to label).

A problem with fine motor may be indicated if a child displays the following difficulties:

1. Difficulty when trying to pick up small objects;
2. Poor formation of letters and untidy spacing of words;
3. Problem with cutting on a line or colouring within lines;
4. Difficulty imitating precise body movements;
5. Gross errors when judging;
6. Problems when trying to use hands cooperatively.

A number of strategies which may be of value are presented for classroom use.

Suggested Strategies

Fine motor coordination: the ability to control and coordinate the small muscles of the body.

Remedial Objective: to correct fine motor disabilities related to eye-hand coordination, ocular control, ocular tracking, visual motor speed, and perceptual motor matching.

Prescriptive teaching strategy 51:

Children sit a short distance apart and roll a ball back and forth. This is a preliminary activity to develop proficiency in visual tracking.

Prescriptive teaching strategy 52:

Bean bags can be the beginning objects for catching activities; they are easy to catch and hold. Instruct two children to kneel with a distance of three feet between them and throw a bean bag back and forth. When they are able to do this competently they can stand and do the same activity. Gradually the distance between the two children is increased.

Prescriptive teaching strategy 53:

Ask the child to throw a ball toward a distant target, such as a wastebasket placed on the other side of the room. As accuracy increases, containers of progressively smaller sizes could be introduced. For motivation, scoring could be linked to container size.

Prescriptive teaching strategy 54:

Any of the ball games, such as volleyball, basketball or handball, can be used to further develop the skills of throwing and catching.

Prescriptive teaching strategy 55:

In ocular pursuit, the child is required to follow a moving object with his eyes. The object could be a person walking, a pencil moving across a page, a ball rolling across the floor or suspended in the air, or a beam of light moving in a dark room.

Prescriptive teaching strategy 56:

Strategy 55 is modified and refined such that a card with a number or letter affixed is rotated in a circular motion. The child is asked to track the moving card and to name the letter or number.

Prescriptive teaching strategy 57:

The teacher writes letters and numbers in the air and the child, focussing his eyes on the teacher's finger movements, tries to identify the letter or number.

Prescriptive teaching strategy 58:

Ask the child to lace with a shoelace or coloured string around various dot designs punched on cardboard. An obvious extension of this activity is shoe tying.

Prescriptive teaching strategy 59:

Pictures can also be completed by the child in a dot-to-dot fashion. The dots are numbered or lettered to indicate the sequence to be followed.

Prescriptive teaching strategy 60:

Cutting activities are recommended for developing fine motor coordination. The child could cut along straight lines, progress to circles, and finally cut out pictures. The children can trace the lines and pictures before they cut them out. Colouring the pictures provides further practice in eye-hand coordination and ocular pursuit.

Prescriptive teaching strategy 61:

Forming patterns with coloured blocks, and stringing beads, macaroni and buttons of various sizes are sometimes worthwhile activities.

Prescriptive teaching strategy 62:

Instruct the child to follow a set course between parallel lines. The lines could be about one inch apart at first and the distance between them gradually decreased. The sets of parallel lines could represent familiar objects, i.e., the outline of a triangle or rabbit.

Prescriptive teaching strategy 63:

The teacher draws a geometric design on the board and the child traces it. Start with a circle and progress to more complex designs. After he becomes proficient at tracing designs, he draws them on his own. Note: tracing here means to draw over existing lines.

Prescriptive teaching strategy 64:

Simple puzzles are useful in developing fine motor coordination. Magazine pictures can be cut up to make puzzles.

Prescriptive teaching strategy 65:

Have the child reproduce simple geometric patterns on a pegboard. The child may reproduce a design presented by the teacher in the form of a drawing on his pegboard.

4/Visual Perception

The visual perceptual area is replete with terms which are invoked to describe various types of dysfunction. Problems related to visual acuity, figure-ground differentiation, visual memory, visual sequential memory, visual motor memory, spatial relations, visual discrimination (size, colour, shape, position in space), eye-hand coordination and a host of others are bandied about. When one begins to review literature related to visual perception one is inundated with terminology.

It would seem apposite at this point to begin sorting through the terminology in the hope of superimposing order. Consequently, this introduction selectively will define and describe aspects of visual perception which the writers consider to be relevant to teaching.

Visual Acuity

The term visual acuity occasionally is used when describing children who have visual perceptual problems. In a strict sense, however, visual acuity refers to sharpness of vision, that is, how well does the child see? If a child has a visual problem of this variety, referral should be made immediately to a school nurse or ophthalmologist. Various behavioural signs help to alert the teacher that a child is experiencing problems with vision.

The National Society for the Prevention of Blindness (1972) has presented a list of classroom indicators of visual problems.

Behaviour:
Rubs eyes excessively;
Shuts or covers one eye, tilts head or thrusts head forward;
Has difficulty in reading or in other work requiring close use of the eyes;
Blinks more than usual or is irritable when doing close work;
Holds books close to eyes;
Is unable to see distant things clearly;
Squints eyelids together or frowns;

18

Appearance:
Crossed eyes;
Red-rimmed, encrusted or swollen eyelids;
Inflamed or watery eyes;
Recurring styes;

Complaints:
Eyes itch, burn or feel scratchy;
Cannot see well;
Dizziness, headaches or nausea following close eye work;
Blurred or double vision.

Such signs singularly or in combination point toward a visual problem. The existence of such a problem may be verified by the school nurse, often by means of the Snellen Chart or the E Chart. These are commonly employed as screening devices.

If the diagnosis is made that the child has a visual problem that cannot be ameliorated by corrective lens, the teacher should make reference to any one of the many references available (such as Barraga, 1976; Bishop, 1971) which relate to teaching partially sighted children. Problems of eye and ear which relate to the receptive process in the sensory organs rather than the interpretation of the sensory data open a large area of research and remediation which is tangential to the thrust of this handbook on learning disabilities.

Visual Discrimination

Visual discrimination is the ability to notice differences between stimuli presented to the visual channel. If you distinguish *p* as different from *q*, *b*, from *d* you are demonstrating competency in visual discrimination involving position in space. If you can arrange hues in serial order from pink to scarlet, you are discriminating colour. Similarly, if you can decide accurately in which order to nest plastic cups of different sizes by looking at them, you are performing size discrimination. Finally, if you see *h* as different from *k*, and *m* as different from *n*, you are well on the way to discriminating shape. From these examples we see that visual discrimination is the ability to detect differences whether they be of position, colour, size, shape or pattern.

In a learning sense, visual discrimination is a key perceptual ability. The ability to differentiate between letters, words and numbers is a functional requisite when approaching reading, spelling, writing and arithmetic. Without such abilities learning is virtually impossible. Barrett (1965) in a study of visual discrimination tasks as a prediction of first grade reading achievement concluded that three visual discrimination tasks make the strongest contribution in such a prediction: (1) the ability to read letters and numbers; (2) the ability to copy geometric patterns; and (3) the ability to match printed words.

Comprehension notwithstanding, reading is basically a matching process in which elements of sounds are matched with marks on paper. This phoneme-grapheme match is problem-ridden without accurate auditory and visual perceptual functioning. Visual discrimination is a key aspect of the matching process. It is obvious that visual discrimination plays a major role in the reading process.

For the child who finds it difficult to make visual discriminations, reading problems are many. Johnson and Myklebust (1967) present a number of reading problems which are frequently encountered. They will serve as a framework to help guide you in observing your students.

1. The child often confuses letters and words which are similar and they fail to note internal detail (i.e., *bag* for *beg*);
2. Their rate of perception is slow (i.e., reading is a slow and cumbersome process);
3. They have reversal tendencies (i.e., tending to read *dig* for *big*; *clam* for *calm*);
4. They tend to invert (i.e., misuse *u* for *n*, *m* for *w*).

In a similar manner, the child who has a problem with visual discrimination finds writing, spelling and mathematics difficult. Reversal and inversion tendencies which characterize reading performance express themselves in mathematics as well with 397 as 793, and 9 seen as 6. Drawing is also inferior, lacking detail and good form.

Visual Figure-Ground

Visual figure-ground distortion relates to the lack of ability to clearly perceive a figure as distinct from its background; that is, the inability to meaningfully perceive a foreground and a background in a differentiated manner rather than as inextricably bound together. The shifting or alternating of ascendant views which one experiences when trying to solve problems involving three-dimensional figures, such as a three-dimensional drawing of a square figure, provides a reasonable analogy to figure-ground distortion.

According to Gearheart (1973), the ability to separate figure from ground equates concentration or focus on items of major importance while relegating less important environmental aspects to the background. Although one does not lose all awareness of the background, it is given much lower precedence in the field of consciousness.

Although it is a relatively simple matter to define the term "figure-ground" in a circumspect fashion, the difficulties caused by figure-ground confusion are not so easily treated. A figure-ground problem destroys the organization of one's perceptual field and with this loss of perceptual stability comes a host of learning difficulties. Visual figure-ground problems confound with perceptual functioning of visual memory, spatial relations, and visual discrimination. Chalfant and Flathouse (1971) express the predominant theme of figure-ground research stating that high distractibility, short attention span, inability to follow directions, clumsiness and reading disability relate to figure-ground disturbance.

Many tests have been developed to detect figure-ground problems. Such tests as the *Children's Embedded Figures Test* (CEFT) and the *Illinois Test of Psycholinguistic Abilities* (ITPA) instruct the subject to locate a hidden figure from a series of backgrounds which become progressively more embedding. It is often the case that such tests are not readily available to the teacher and, as a consequence, observation becomes critically important.

In addition to the list of disabilities commonly ascribed to children with visual perceptual problems, the child experiencing figure-ground distortion will exhibit some behaviours that distinctly relate to his problem. Some of the more frequent problems are presented:

1. Difficulty in selecting his name from a group of names;
2. Lack of sensitivity to boundaries when painting and colouring;
3. Difficulty in recognizing himself in a group photo;
4. Slowness in completing picture puzzles;
5. Failure to detect missing parts in a photo or drawing;
6. Lack of detail in verbal descriptions;
7. Inability to pick out or trace around one figure when two or more overlap.

Remedial suggestions related to figure-ground distortion are presented later in this chapter.

Spatial Relations

As is true with visual figure-ground, there is some degree of commonality in definitions which have been presented for spatial relations. According to Gearheart (1973) spatial relations is the ability to recognize the position of objects in relation to one another and to the observer as well. Lerner (1976) states that this dimension of visual functioning implies the perception of a symbol or object and its relative position to other surrounding entities. In reading, words must be seen as separate entities surrounded by space.

Money (1962) has stated that the perceiver is confronted with two aspects of spatial relations—position (directionality) and spacing (distances between objects). As pointed out by Johnson and Myklebust (1967), there are in English numerous letters which are similar in general configuration and differ as to sound and meaning solely by the way in which they rotate and orientate relative to the page. For example, *u* and *n* are merely inverted versions of the same symbol. Consider this example:

He hit the *d*uck.
He hit the *p*uck.
He hit the *b*uck.

In the absence of context cues it is the spatial relationship between the initial consonant *d, p, b* and the rest of the word which determines meaning.

At this point it must be conceded that spatial relations represent a number of aspects of visual functioning in combination rather than a discrete perceptual ability. Visual discrimination and directionality are most certainly part of the concept.

A dysfunction in spatial relation sometimes is reflected in a writing disability. As the child attempts to print a sentence, he may find it difficult to judge the amount of space to leave between letters and words. He may print sentences such as: *Iwantagonow.* or *Iwa nta g onow.*

The importance of space in the understanding of numbers and arithmetic is well recognized. Up-down, high-low, near-far, beginning-end and over-under are basic concepts when approaching the number system and operations involving it.

Visual Memory

The role of memory in human learning has been recognized for centuries. It has been researched under a variety of subtitles and facets: imagery, storage, retrieval, serial and free recall, memory span, short-term memory and long-term memory. We shall limit our present discussion to visual memory while conceding that auditory memory is equally important to the learning process. The key role of auditory memory and the detrimental effect of deficiencies in this area are presented later in the discussion of auditory perceptual dysfunction.

The ability to precisely recall previous visual experiences is essential to most of the things which we do and attempt to learn during our school experience. Problems related to visual memory impede the child early in his formal learning because basic work with both numbers and letters involves memory. If learning is to be cumulative, arithmetic and language symbols must be stored efficiently enough that they may be revisualized—the child must remember how they appeared.

One must be careful to differentiate between the child who does not remember and the child who cannot remember. Buckhout (1975), demonstrating the inability of eye witnesses to several accidents to accurately report what they had seen, pointed out a number of factors which limit a person's ability to remember visual events. Some of these factors have meaning for the teacher. One implication of his research is that stimuli must be perceived as having some importance in order to facilitate learning. There must be a reason for remembering; the event must have meaning. Besides being significant, the things to be remembered must not be so heavily laden with unnecessary detail that the essentials are lost. As teachers we must carefully sort out pseudo-memory problems, rather than hastily conclude that a learning disability exists.

Although visual memory is pervasive to the learning process, it is of heightened importance in the reading process: at first in learning the alphabet, later in the development of a sight vocabulary. For the child with a severe memory problem, a word which has been previously taught must be learned anew on each occasion that it is encountered. As a consequence, the process of reading picks up a negative valence which often becomes generalized to the entire learning process.

The teacher must be on the lookout for persistent and obstinate problems in memory. Some words invite learning and are readily grasped. Words which are valued and evoke imagery for the child, such as "ghost," "tiger" and "snowman," require less concerted study of structure and detail than words such as "rather," "could" and "then." Boring words generally require more exposure for learning to occur. The child with a true memory problem has problems *with words*, not just the less interesting words.

Chalfant and Scheffelin (1969) have stated that memory skills in reading include the following:

1. The ability to retain impressions or traces of visual and auditory stimuli;
2. The ability to make comparisons with past auditory and visual experiences;
3. The ability to store and retrieve grapheme-phoneme correspondences.

Given that reading is, at its simplest level, the ability to match units of sound with marks on paper, a problem can exist if the child has difficulty recalling either the visual or auditory component. In the case of visual memory dysfunction, the child may be unable to recognize specific letters and words.

As noted by Wallace and McLoughlin (1975), the storage and retrieval components of the memory process have relevance to the discussion of learning problems. The child who has difficulty remembering "g," for instance, is experiencing retrieval problems. Memory for the letter is dependent upon adequate storage; consequently, it is often difficult to determine the exact point where the memory process has broken down.

The inability to revisualize the image of a word indicates a problem of memory; the ability to remember the letters but not their position in the structure of the word is indicative of sequential memory dysfunction. Or, more simply stated, sequential memory refers to memory for order, i.e., the serial position of the letters in a word or of words in a sentence. A deficit related to visual sequential memory often results in scrambled words such as *clam* for *calm* or *silm* for *slim*. Johnson and Myklebust (1967) state that such problems are common among learning disabled children and often persist longer than other reading problems. If sequential memory is considered in terms of other curriculum aspects, nowhere does a deficit of this type stand out so boldly as in spelling.

One further aspect of memory which has received much attention is motor memory. Fernald (1943) pointed out that in order to spell a word the child must know every detail of the word form. This, she stated, is a more complex task than recognizing the word, as is the case in reading. If a child has a memory problem, it is often the case that he has problems when confronted with the additional skills required for spelling. According to Fernald, in order to write a word the student must remember the kinesthetic "feel" of the word, a sequential movement pattern of letters. The Fernald technique, which is a tracing approach to spelling problems, has been one of the most effective methods which have been developed to assist with motor memory problems.

Major trends in remedial programs directed toward memory problems involve repetition, multisensory presentations, and the use of memory aids known as "mnemonic devices." The ensuing remedial strategies incorporate these techniques.

Suggested Strategies

Visual discrimination: the ability to differentiate between stimuli on the basis of various visibly observable attributes such as size, shape and colour.

Remedial Objective: to teach children to recognize differences and similarities between objects. This is considered a prerequisite to discrimination between words in the reading process.

Prescriptive teaching strategy 66:
Use an assortment of coloured geometric shapes. Instruct the children to group them using different frames of reference (i.e., all the red shapes, all the triangles, all the small shapes).

Prescriptive teaching strategy 67:

Collect a set of different sizes and colours of a designated geometric shape (i.e., triangle). Ask the child to point out similarities and differences within the set.

Prescriptive teaching strategy 68:

Give each child a selection of coloured geometric forms. The teacher holds up a card with a particular coloured shape, for example, a red circle. The child has to select a red circle from his collection. If there is more than one red circle in his collection, he has to select the one which matches most closely the one that is on the card.

Prescriptive teaching strategy 69:

Provide exercise sheets of numbers or letters. The first component of each row is underlined. The child has to proceed along the row and underline the items which are the same as the first one.

Prescriptive teaching strategy 70:

This is an extension of strategy 69, except this time words are used. The distractor words would have the initial consonant changed or might have the order of letters reversed, for example, *hit*—bit tih pit hit his hit.

Prescriptive teaching strategy 71:

Using beads of different colours and shapes, the teacher makes a specific design on a string. The child is given a piece of string and some beads and is asked to duplicate the teacher's design.

Prescriptive teaching strategy 72:

Using paint, coloured bottles and lids of varying sizes. Separate the two and have the child match the bottles and lids of the same colour. A variation of this would be to use nuts and bolts.

Prescriptive teaching strategy 73:

Select an assortment of objects and outline their shapes on paper. After selecting an object the child is asked to find where it fits on the sheet of traced forms.

Prescriptive teaching strategy 74:

Give the child a number of rectangles which are the same width, but which differ in length. Have him arrange them in order from the shortest to the longest. The finished product resembles a set of steps.

Prescriptive teaching strategy 75:

The child is given a number of cards with one word written on each card. A number of boxes with two letters written on the front of them are provided. The child has to sort the word cards into the appropriate boxes matching the last two letters in the words with the letters appearing on the boxes.

Prescriptive teaching strategy 76:

Prepare two identical sets of cards with each card containing one word. Shuffle the cards and have the children match the decks. Commercial cards may also be used—suit, number, colour.

Prescriptive teaching strategy 77:

Write a list of words on the left side of a page. Write the same words on the right side of the page in a scrambled order. Ask the child to match the words by drawing lines from one column to the other. This can also be done with pictures which may be more suitable for younger children.

Prescriptive teaching strategy 78:

Ask the child to comprise a list of designated objects, i.e.: (a) all the things that are smaller than a book; (b) bigger than he is; (c) round; and (d) square.

Visual figure-ground: the ability to distinguish between the background and the foreground of a visual stimulus.

Remedial Objective: to teach the child to respond differentially to various aspects of a visual presentation.

Prescriptive teaching strategy 79:

Suggest categories of objects for the child to visually select, such as all the green things or all the circular things in the room.

Prescriptive teaching strategy 80:

Sorting activities can be a remediational strategy for problems in visual figure-ground. Everyday objects are of value: sorting knives, forks and spoons; crayons and pencils; and triangles, circles and squares.

Prescriptive teaching strategy 81:

Present the child with a picture and ask him to identify specific objects, such as the barn in the field behind the fence. Family photographs could also be utilized.

Prescriptive teaching strategy 82:

Instruct the child to cut out a particular object from a picture. At first, the objects might be outlined by the teacher with a coloured pencil.

Prescriptive teaching strategy 83:

Using laces or coloured wool, have the child lace a design which has been traced on cardboard.

Prescriptive teaching strategy 84:

Present the child with a pegboard design constructed from coloured rubber bands. On his pegboard the child has to copy the design. Also he could copy progressively more complex designs presented in various pictorial backgrounds.

Prescriptive teaching strategy 85:

Colouring is beneficial for remediation of figure-ground difficulties. In colouring, the child is required to locate the various body parts and articles of clothing if he is to colour them appropriately. The child could trace the outline with his crayon first, before beginning the actual colouring.

Prescriptive teaching strategy 86:

Present the child with a set of similar pictures, of which two are identical. The child has to find the two which are identical.

Prescriptive teaching strategy 87:

Each child is given a picture in which there are some hidden figures. He attempts to be the first to find all the hidden figures.

Prescriptive teaching strategy 88:

Draw overlapping figures, for example, a circle and a square. Have the child outline each shape with a different coloured pencil.

Prescriptive teaching strategy 89:

Jigsaw puzzles of all sorts are quite effective. The child has to assemble the pieces into a meaningful picture. The starting puzzles should have good figure-ground contrast.

Prescriptive teaching strategy 90:

All sorts of connect-the-dot activities are appropriate for helping to remediate difficulties with figure-ground. When the picture is completed it could be coloured.

Prescriptive teaching strategy 91:

Select a magazine picture and cut out a part of it. Place the part which has been cut out with several other pieces of paper which are identical in shape but are incorrect in terms of completing the picture. Have the child choose and fit the appropriate piece into the picture.

Spatial relations: the ability to locate an object in relation to surrounding objects.

Remedial Objective: to familiarize the child with spatial relationships: up-down, top-bottom, over-under, high-low, front-back, beginning-end, across.

Prescriptive teaching strategy 92:

Ask the child to find the top, bottom, sides and back of selected objects. The objects may be presented in atypical positions such as upside-down.

Prescriptive teaching strategy 93:

The child attempts to find objects in the classroom by following the teacher's verbal directions, i.e., find the small box on the top shelf behind you.

Prescriptive teaching strategy 94:

Set up an obstacle course. The teacher directs the child to go over, under and around certain objects in order to successfully negotiate the course.

Prescriptive teaching strategy 95:

Give the child a paper which contains pictures of a variety of objects. Draw a line horizontally across the paper and ask the child to identify objects above and below the line. Also, the teacher could name an object and have the child tell whether it is above or below the line.

Prescriptive teaching strategy 96:

One child hides an object and another child has to discover where the object is by asking questions. If the child discovers the location of the missing object, he is given the opportunity to hide it.

Prescriptive teaching strategy 97:

After explaining what is meant by the word "middle" or "centre," have one child examine another child's face to locate its centre. Present pictures of objects, such as a clock, a seesaw and a circle and have the children determine the centre.

Prescriptive teaching strategy 98:
The teacher arranges an uneven number of objects in a row, tells the child that one of these is in the middle position and asks him to identify it.

Prescriptive teaching strategy 99:
Assist the children in placing North, South, East and West on a map of Canada. Instruct the child to indicate the direction of various centres in relationship to the school.

Prescriptive teaching strategy 100:
Have the student examine pictures depicting objects placed in various positions. Using real objects identical to the ones depicted in the pictures, have the child arrange them to match the pictures.

Prescriptive teaching strategy 101:
Draw five identical objects in various spatial positions.

b:　d p b q

The child is requested to find the object whose position in space matches the first object from among the four remaining objects.

Visual memory: the ability to process, store and retrieve visually presented information.
Remedial Objective: to help the child learn the required skills for reading and manipulating abstract symbols.

Prescriptive teaching strategy 102:
Place four different objects on the child's desk and let him observe them for a few seconds. Then request him to close his eyes while you remove one of the objects. The child has to tell which object is missing when he opens his eyes. A variation of this would be to place the missing object in a group of other objects and have the child try to identify it. Difficulty increases as the number of objects is increased.

Prescriptive teaching strategy 103:
Have the child close his eyes and describe where a teacher-named object is in relation to surrounding objects.

Prescriptive teaching strategy 104:

Present a picture briefly. Then, instruct the child to find the picture from among a group of pictures. A modification of this procedure involving recall rather than recognition would be to have the child reproduce the picture on paper.

Prescriptive teaching strategy 105:

The child is briefly exposed to a segment of a picture. Next, he is given the total picture, and he has to determine which section of the picture he has just seen.

Prescriptive teaching strategy 106:

Ask the child to close his eyes and tell where certain other children are seated—who sits behind? in front of? across from? He could also be given a seating plan to fill in from memory.

Prescriptive teaching strategy 107:

The child is given a number of objects to carefully examine before they are placed in a paper bag. He inserts his hand and grasps an object and determines which object he is touching through visual memory.

Prescriptive teaching strategy 108:

The student is given four pictures which tell a story when they are placed in proper sequence. The cards are shuffled and presented to the child who must arrange them in proper sequence. This activity could be performed with abstract designs making it more a test of visual memory.

Prescriptive teaching strategy 109:

The pupil watches another child proceed through a maze. He must duplicate the movements of the first child through the maze.

Prescriptive teaching strategy 110:

Present the child with a nonsense word (razak). Scramble the letters and have him arrange them in the appropriate sequence. It is advisable to use nonsense words in that it guards against being able to spell the word from prior exposure.

Prescriptive teaching strategy 111:

A group of three letters is covered and placed before the student. The teacher holds up a card which contains one of the letters. When the card is taken away, the letters are revealed and the child has to discover the one which has been presented. This activity can later be extended to include whole words, nonsense syllables, etc.

Prescriptive teaching strategy 112:

The child is presented with a five-word sentence. He looks at it for a specified time, and then closes his eyes while the teacher removes one word. Context provides an additional cue for the child as he attempts to recall the missing word. Later, the whole sentence could be taken away and the child asked to recall it.

Prescriptive teaching strategy 113:

Briefly expose a complete picture to the child and then show him the same picture with a part missing. The child has to recall and draw the missing part. Subsequent pictures would have more parts missing and finally the child would be required to draw the complete picture.

Prescriptive teaching strategy 114:

Numbered dot-to-dot pictures require that the child know numbers and be able to recall them in sequential order to correctly complete the picture. Difficulty is increased when larger numbers of dots are presented and the starting number is greater than ten.

Prescriptive teaching strategy 115:

On cards, write simple commands that the child can easily carry out. Have him read the information on the card and carry out the commands without referring to the cards again.

5 / Auditory Perception

Audition is another sensory modality which has significance for learning. Three important components of audition which will be examined in this chapter are auditory acuity, auditory discrimination and auditory memory.

Auditory acuity refers to the faintest sound an individual can hear (Davis, 1970). The observation of children in the classroom for signs of hearing loss and the administration of informal tests of auditory acuity are the initial steps in auditory assessment. Several texts (Carter and McGinnis, 1970; Dechant, 1968; Miller, 1973) reveal that the teacher may detect difficulties in auditory acuity by sensitizing himself to a number of behavioural cues displayed by the child, such as:

1. Not responding when called to answer a question;
2. Listening with a blank or tense facial expression or tilting the head while listening;
3. Ignoring directions, appearing to be inattentive, and often asking to have words or phrases repeated;
4. Articulating sounds poorly.

The teacher should also be sensitive to physical signs which may relate to problems in auditory acuity. Some of these include recent injury to the ears, discharge from the ear, reports of frequent earaches, frequent colds and sinus infections, and complaints of noises in the ear or head.

Auditory Acuity

Two informal auditory acuity tests are the *whisper test* and the *ticking-watch test*, both of which should be administered to the child suspected of having a hearing deficit. Since the whisper and conversational voice represent sounds that are important for students to hear, it is essential to include assessments of these two qualities of the spoken voice. The ticking-watch test, which assesses the ability to hear high frequency sounds, is included because of its greater sensitivity to early detection of a hearing deficit. According to Davis (1970), the ticking-watch test is "useful because loss of hearing often begins with a loss of sensitivity for high frequencies."

For rapid and approximate testing, the crude but time-honoured methods—the whisper test and ticking-watch test—will be described. Although descriptions of these two preliminary auditory examinations appear in a number of publications, Farrald and Schamber (1973) include the most detail. Their description of the procedure for administering the whisper test is as follows:

> Line up several children (usually four or five) approximately five feet from the examiner and facing away from the examiner. Again, testing should be done in a quiet room and in a room with a minimum of distractions. The examiner remains in the same spot behind the children and gives directions in a low, distinct tone of voice. The directions should be very simple. Watch the children and note those who hesitate, who watch others to see what they do, who look back at the examiner or those who fail to follow direction. The children move ahead slowly until they are unable to hear the whisper. If a child functions well at twenty feet, his hearing is likely to be within normal limits. Another version of this test is to have the children stand twenty feet away from the examiner, with one ear turned away from the examiner. The examiner whispers (or says in a soft, distinct tone) single words which the child attempts to repeat. If the child is unable to perform adequately, the examiner moves forward until the responses are correct. Each ear is, of course, examined separately.

In testing the child's ability to hear conversational voice, the description of the procedure for the whisper test can be used as a guideline. Inherent in these crude assessment procedures are at least two questionable assumptions: first, that testing can be conducted in a quiet room in which the walls do not reflect sound; second, that one individual's voice is as easy to understand as another's.

Davis (1970) claims that the whisper test has an advantage over the conversational voice test because voice intensity is difficult to standardize. The whisper on the other hand can be standardized in intensity or "loudness" by whispering only at the end of an expiration. A word of caution in using these two crude tests is that performance can be improved with training. Hirsh (1970) contends that the young child during initial testing will not automatically respond to levels of sound that are as low as those to which he will respond after some experience training. The performance of the child in either hearing test is expressed as a ratio to the performance of children with "normal" auditory acuity.

On the average, a child with normal hearing just understands the whispered voice at twenty feet. If we must come within ten feet of a child before he can understand a whisper, we say that his hearing is 10/20, meaning that he can just understand at ten feet a whisper that the average child understands at twenty feet. The analogy to the Snellen Chart for visual acuity is obvious (Davis, 1970).

The ticking-watch test, with its sensitivity to hearing loss at higher frequencies, is described below:

> Have the child stand with one ear toward the examiner and have him place his finger in the other ear. Screen the child's head with a card so that the child cannot see the watch. Hold the watch close to the child's ear and gradually move it away until he can no longer hear it. Then hold the watch forty-eight inches from the child's ear and gradually move closer until the child hears the watch ticking. The average child should be able to hear the watch tick at a distance of approximately forty-eight inches. If the average of the two measures is less than twenty inches, the child should be referred for in-depth testing. (A loud-ticking watch such as the Ingersol or the Westclox Pocket Ben should be used.) Be sure the testing is done in a quiet room (Farrald and Schamber, 1973).

A possible limitation of the ticking-watch test is the assumption that ticks from different watches are identical. Therefore, the same watch should be used for repeated testing of the child.

These informal techniques serve to alert the teacher to aspects of behaviour that he may not have otherwise considered in detecting and assessing the hearing impairment, and allow for the preparation of a referral. A suspected hearing loss should be discussed with the student's parents so that they may, in turn, make an appropriate referral to a hearing specialist.

The authors contend that the special education teacher is generally not equipped to deal with auditory acuity problems but does play, nonetheless, a significant role in the early detection of hearing problems. The results of the whisper and ticking-watch tests should be noted, together with observations of the child's behaviour. Particular attention should be given to symptoms that are frequently manifested by the child and that rarely occur among his classmates.

Auditory Discrimination

In addition to auditory acuity, the child must develop skills in discriminating or distinguishing one sound from another. The first aspect of auditory discrimination to consider is the ability to locate the source or direction of the sound. There is practical utility and even "safety value" attached to auditory spatial discrimination. The child pedestrian is safer, for example, if he can determine whether a car is approaching him from the right or the left. Auditory spatial discrimination, therefore, should be included in a discussion of auditory discrimination.

Sound localization in the horizontal plane—the plane which is parallel to the ground and which passes through the ears—will be examined because the majority of sounds we have to locate in everyday life, such as voices and automobile sounds, occur in this plane. What are the possible cues that the child uses in locating these sources of sounds? Time can function as a cue to the right-left localization of sound. For example, if a signal is sound at the right of the student in the horizontal plane, he will probably report the source as being at the "right" rather than at the "left" because the sound will reach the right ear sooner than it will reach the left ear. Similarly, for the same reason, a signal emitted at the left of the child will be reported to be at the "left" rather than at the "right" because the sound reaches the left ear first (Murch, 1973). Thurlow (1971) reported that "for each centimetre of difference in the distance to the two ears, there will be a time difference of about .029 msec." It can be seen, therefore, that the difference reaches a maximum when the sound source is directly opposite one ear.

A second "cue" for determining left-right localization of a stimulus sound is the intensity or "loudness" difference at the two ears. The head acts as a barrier in lessening the perceived intensity of the sound farthest away from the source. This causes a "differential effect" such that the auditory stimulus appears "louder" at one of the ears than at the other. As with the time cue, the difference in the intensity of the sound tends to be greatest when the source is nearly opposite one ear.

It is more difficult for the child to determine the location of sounds that are in front of or behind him. A student who is experiencing difficulties in locating the position of such sounds can partially resolve ambiguities in temporal or intensity cues by using head movements to maximize the effectiveness of these two cues (Murch, 1973; Thurlow, 1971). Suggested procedures for teaching children with sound localization problems:

1. Use musical instruments or pots and pans to produce a visible source of sound;
2. Turn the child's head toward the sound source;
3. Make the sound source visible to the child when he turns his head in the direction of the sound (Faas, 1976).

According to Carhart (1960), there are three main types of auditory discriminations required in everyday life. The first—distinguishing between sounds which are highly dissimilar—is known as *gross auditory discrimination*. It is relatively easy, for example, to distinguish the sound of a siren from that of an automobile horn, or the crying of a child from the barking of a dog. The baby initially learns gross auditory discriminations based on a small number of sounds before he understands any of the words spoken to him, e.g., distinguishing affection from disapproval by the sound of his mother's voice.

The second type, *simple speech discrimination*, is recognition of simple words or phrases under favourable listening conditions, that is, in a quiet place and in close proximity to the speaker. The infant soon reaches the stage of understanding single words such as "Daddy" and short phrases or sentences such as, "Come to Mummy."

Difficult speech discrimination is the recognition of words and sentences under adverse listening conditions of either or both of two types. The recognition of words under a condition of a disturbing background noise, such as classmates constructively involved in a group project, will require "masking out" of the irrelevant noise. The second unfavourable listening condition involves the recognition of unfamiliar words in the absence of contextual cues. For example, we often ask to have an unfamiliar name spelled to ascertain if we heard it correctly.

Some children experience difficulty with certain sounds (/b/, /t/, /sl/) regardless of their position in a word, while other children have problems with only initial or final consonant sounds. Spache and Spache (1973) report that performance in auditory discrimination activities is the best single predictor of first grade reading success. Wallace and McLoughlin (1975) suggest three indicators which may predict later difficulties in distinguishing the sounds of letters. These are: distinguishing between loud and soft sounds; rhyming, because it requires the ability to perceive auditory similarities in words; and distinguishing between animal and vehicle sounds. According to Faas (1976), children with auditory problems will have difficulty in:

1. Distinguishing nonlanguage from language sounds;
2. Distinguishing between sounds which differ in pitch, loudness or duration;
3. Determining if phrases or sentences are the same or different;
4. Determining if blended sounds are the same or different;
5. Determining if the initial, medial or final sounds of two words are the same or different, e.g., tin - pin, mit - met, car - can;
6. Identifying the word that begins/ends with a certain letter sound from among a list of words read aloud.

Auditory discrimination is obviously very important to the student learning to read, since he must distinguish between similar sounds before he can accurately reproduce these sounds himself. A student must also have the ability to mask out extraneous noises so that he can hear what the teacher or another student is saying. Therefore, any student who has a number of difficulties with auditory discrimination activities should be given an auditory discrimination test.

The best known and most widely used test is Wepman's *Auditory Discrimination Test*. This is an individual test in which the examiner pronounces a number of pairs of words that are either identical or alike except for one phoneme, e.g., lack - lock and tub - tug. The student responds by indicating whether the two words are the same or different.

When giving the Auditory Discrimination Test, it is important for the student to understand that "same" and "different" refer to the sounds of the words and not to the meanings of the words. If a student does poorly, it is also a good idea to wait several days and give the same test again to insure that the results of the first administration were valid. If, in giving the test, you find that many students fail, you should consider having a sample of that group tested by another person to ensure that your pronunciation is not at fault.

Although originally designed as an individual test, it may be given in a group situation. In this case students are given an answer sheet numbered in correspondence with each pair of words on the test. As the words are pronounced, the student writes a (−) for a pair of words that are different and a (+) for words that are the same. Recording the test words on tape and giving the test via a tape recorder insures more accurate results.

Keir (cited in White, Lefroy and Weston, 1975) maintains that the child's response in a paired-words test depends on correctly saying the words silently to himself. Keir, therefore, prefers assessments which require the child to repeat aloud the word pronounced by the examiner, his rationale being that if a child can correctly repeat two different words, for example, bat - pat, then he can discriminate between the /b/ and /p/ sounds. It does seem reasonable that if a child can correctly pronounce words that are either the same or different, then he demonstrates ability to discriminate them auditorily. Since the expressive function of repeating a word, however, could interfere with the assessment of the ability to discriminate sounds, Keir's criticism appears to be questionable. With this in mind, it is conceivable that a child could consistently and correctly tell whether word pairs are the same or different yet pronounce the words incorrectly. The weakness of Keir's hypothesis seems to be that the pupil's inability to correctly articulate paired words could represent a deficit in expression rather than auditory discrimination.

Auditory Figure-Ground

Auditory figure-ground should be considered in the context of auditory discrimination. This ability can be conceptualized as the "skill of selecting and attending to relevant auditory stimuli" (Wallace and McLoughlin, 1975). This means that the child must not only filter out distracting stimuli but must learn also how to readily change his focus of attention.

Accordingly, a student competent in figure-ground discrimination demonstrates ability to focus attention on a teacher's directions in a noisy room.

It will undoubtedly be recognized that auditory discrimination is involved in auditory figure-ground ability and that at least two auditory stimuli must be present for its investigaiton. Which of the two stimuli constitutes figure or ground is determined by the particular *context* in which they occur. A distinction can be made between the testing procedures for auditory figure-ground and auditory discrimination. In auditory figure-ground assessment, the child is required to distinguish between two simultaneously presented auditory stimuli (Thurlow, 1971). As an illustration, the teacher taps on a desk while simultaneously bunching or crackling a piece of cellophane in her other hand. The student is asked to "select and attend" to the taps and to demonstrate this in a performance measure of a count or tally while screening out the cracking sound. In the testing procedure for auditory discrimination ability, such as in a paired-words test, only one auditory stimulus (word) is presented at a time.

In discussing the testing of auditory discrimination, Sanders (1971) suggests a systematic hierarchy to be followed in diagnosing the child. Vowel sound discrimination should be tested first. The following list of words illustrates the way in which multiple choice lists can be constructed to test most vowels:

rot:	rat	rot	rut
pen:	pin	pen	pan

Note that it is desirable to have the words identical except for the vowels. If more than one letter in the words is different, the words should still be very similar as illustrated by the test item:

been:	born	burn	been

In the sample test question (rot: rat rot rut), the examiner pronounces aloud the word *rot* and the child responds by crossing out the word on his answer sheet that is identical to the spoken word. Only the response alternatives are printed on the answer sheet. When working with very young children, pictures or photographs should be used instead of words. In the test item (pen: pin pen pan), the three response choices of pin, pen and pan would be illustrated by a picture of each of these objects. From this rough-and-ready measure, it should be possible to decide whether auditory training for vowel discrimination is indicated.

According to Sanders's diagnostic model, the next step is to test consonant sound discrimination. The method to be used is similar to the forced choice procedure described for assessing vowel discrimination. In the following test questions, note that the vowels and final consonants are controlled, that is, are identical, while the initial consonants are different:

fill:	will	fill
fall:	wall	fall

Lists could also be prepared to test auditory discrimination of consonants in the medial and final positions of a word. The auditory task could be made more difficult by increasing the selection from which the choice must be made. In this instance, a student might be asked to identify a test word from a group of four response alternatives:

cat:	cat	mat	sat	fat

Although more difficult discriminations are introduced by increasing the number of alternatives in the multiple choice format, one disadvantage of using four response alternatives is that it increases the teacher's difficulty in selecting words that are identical except for one consonant. An advantage of using only two or three response choices is that it allows for a greater number of questions to be included. If selected consonants appear in a number of questions, this increases the likelihood of detecting particular consonants which may be causing difficulty for the listener.

The final step in Sanders's hierarchy is testing auditory discrimination under conditions of noise, that is, the testing of auditory figure-ground. Test materials for assessing the child's ability to discriminate speech in a background of noise can be conveniently made. Using a battery-operated tape recorder, recordings of speech could be simultaneously made in a store, a factory or on a busy street. Simultaneous recordings of speech and "ground" or noise could also be made in the classroom against a background conversation being carried on by the student's friends, or the verbal message could be made against the noise of a radio being played at a comfortable level.

Sanders recommends that sounds to be detected by the student be recorded in their natural settings with the appropriate background noise. This permits the individual to develop an appropriate *auditory set* based on *nonverbal situational cues.* If it is not possible to record the actual test material in its appropriate noise environment, noise may be recorded alone and played separately as a background to the material presented at the time of testing. In the case of voice recordings, the microphone should first be held at a distance of six inches from the speaker, and then at a normal conversational distance of three to four feet. As the microphone is moved further away from the listener, the ability to distinguish between speech and noise becomes increasingly difficult. General guidelines for developing remedial programs in auditory discrimination are:

1. Begin with two sounds which are clearly different (h/k/s);
2. Introduce familiar sounds first;
3. Keep in mind that younger children require longer to absorb sound;

4. Move on to discrimination of finer differences only after the child is able to distinguish between gross sounds (Faas, 1976).

Auditory Memory

Auditory memory, that is, the ability to retain and recall speech sounds, is not well developed in children until the age of nine (Wepman, 1968). A discussion of auditory problems in children would be incomplete without a consideration of both short- and long-term memory. Shiffrin and Atkinson (1969) describe a conceptual mode for human memory. They suggest that auditory information is initially processed through a "receiving station" called the *sensory register*. After the auditory information is received, it may be further processed in different ways. The information may be transmitted to *short-term memory* from the sensory register for immediate use. Dialing a telephone number immediately after being told it would illustrate short-term retention of the information. Because this information is not transmitted or "copied" in the *long-term memory* store, it is subject to rapid forgetting. In addition to being transmitted from the sensory register to short-term memory, the information may also be copied in long-term store for subsequent retrieval and use. "Remembering" a telephone number told to you yesterday would be an example of recall involving long-term memory.

The way in which the auditory input is handled by the internal processing system is determined by what Shiffrin and Atkinson call the *control processes*. Continuing with the telephone example, it may be generally agreed that a person would not be inclined to commit to long-term memory an infrequently used telephone number. A telephone number considered important, however, would be committed to memory by rehearsal or by an appropriate mnemonic device to "guarantee" its being "copied" in long-term store. Since it is easier to code concrete words imaginally with a visual picture or image than it is to commit the auditory message to memory by using a purely verbal code, it is necessary to discuss the role of imagery in an examination of auditory memory. Verbal coding, however, seems preferable to visual imagery for committing abstract words to memory. It would be extremely difficult, for example, to code an abstract term such as "auditory memory" imaginally. The details of a particular child's Hallowe'en costume as described to an individual are more easily committed to the listener's memory through visual rather than verbal coding. That is to say, it would be easier to recall the child's dress by imagining what the child looked like rather than by attempting to remember the words used by the person providing the description.

Fortunately, we do not have to remember hundreds of bits of information to perform each day-to-day activity. It has been hypothesized by Ashby (cited in West and Foster, 1976) that one "stores" only a limited number of bits of information and that memory is facilitated by cues embedded in the environment. In driving a car from point A to point B, a driver would undoubtedly encounter many cues "embedded" in the environment, e.g., road signs of various sorts such as "Turn left for B." In this instance, it appears that his task is made easier because the sign (environmental cue) tells him which way to turn. He does not have to remember which way to turn at this junction but needs only to read the sign and turn left. The response pattern of turning left, however, would have been previously stored internally in long-term memory. Perhaps he might encounter another sign down the road a few miles with an arrow prominently displayed under directions to turn left, thus making it unnecessary for the driver to even know the difference between "left" and "right." But even in this instance he would have to have internalized some information, that is, how to turn the wheel in the direction indicated by the arrow.

Similarly, a recipe need not be committed to memory because of environmentally embedded cues such as a list of ingredients, the proportion for each, and the appropriate temperature and cooking time. As with the driver, we assume that the cook had previously coded in long-term memory certain bits of information, such as telling time, operating a stove, using baking utensils, etc.

The child with auditory memory problems may be unable to retrieve from memory the essential auditory information needed for a response. Because of this, he often makes adaptations in his language, such as:

1. Substituting the sound made by the object for its name, "meow" for the word "cat";
2. Resorting to gestures, pantomime or drawing pictures in response to specific questions;
3. Waiting several seconds before answering;
4. Describing the use of an object rather than giving its name, i.e., "drink" for "glass";
5. Substituting a synonym for the "desired word", i.e., "car" for "automobile";
6. Writing the word instead of saying it (Faas, 1976).

According to Wallace and McLoughlin (1975), children with auditory memory deficits may be unable to remember individual letter sounds or the sequence of sounds within a word. Learning other sequential activities such as days of the week, months of the year, or the alphabet may also be difficult for the child with auditory memory disturbances. The reader is referred to the remedial strategies which follow.

Suggested Strategies

Auditory Discrimination: the ability to recognize different sounds and to distinguish one sound from another.

Remedial Objective: to teach the child the difference between sounds, a functional prerequisite to verbal communication.

Prescriptive teaching strategy 116:

Present the child with two sounds, such as a drum and a bell. Have the child close his eyes while you sound one of the instruments and direct the child to open his eyes and identify the instrument which was struck.

Prescriptive teaching strategy 117:

One child in the group is blindfolded while another child says a few words. The blindfolded child must guess who spoke and if difficulty is encountered, the speaker can say additional words.

Prescriptive teaching strategy 118:

Partially fill covered containers of the same size with a variety of objects such as sand, rice, toothpicks and nails, so that there are two containers for each. Rearrange the position of the containers and ask the child to shake the boxes and determine which sound alike by putting them in pairs.

Prescriptive teaching strategy 119:

Say pairs of words or sounds which may be identical or different—wren, wreath; box, box; bill, ball. Request the child to tell whether the sounds are the same or different. If they are different, ask them to explain the difference.

Prescriptive teaching strategy 120:

Record a series of common everyday sounds and select pictures that go with them. Play a sound and have the child select the picture that goes with it.

Prescriptive teaching strategy 121:

On a musical instrument play high and low notes and have the child tell which notes are "high" and which are "low." If a musical instrument is not available, they could be presented on a tape recorder. This activity is geared to training in pitch discrimination.

Auditory Memory: the ability to store auditorily presented information in memory for recall.

Remedial Objective: to help the child retain prior auditory experiences, so that he can relate them to the present.

Prescriptive teaching strategy 122:

Ask the student to repeat a short sequence of words or numbers after they have been presented. Gradually increase list length.

Prescriptive teaching strategy 123:

Ask the child everyday information questions such as, "Do you have a pet?"; "What colour is it?"; "What is its name?".

Prescriptive teaching strategy 124:

The children are seated around the teacher and are asked to listen very carefully. The teacher selects a child and says, "I need . . . . Would you please get it for me?" The teacher gives the child an appropriate reward for completing the task correctly. If the teacher asks the child to get an object(s) which cannot be brought, the child sits in his chair and informs the teacher that it cannot be brought. The memory aspect of this activity is related to memory for oral instructions.

Prescriptive teaching strategy 125:

The teacher asks the children to close their eyes while she claps out a sequence. She calls on a child to repeat the clapping pattern.

Prescriptive teaching strategy 126:

Select a child to be a storekeeper and another to be a customer. The customer asks for a short list of items. The storekeeper has to remember the list and select the items. Gradually the list is increased as the game progresses.

Prescriptive teaching strategy 127:

Have the children line up in rows of five. The teacher names five objects in the classroom and the first child in each row has to touch each object in order of presentation. Each correct answer scores one point for the team. When the first child is finished, he goes to the end of the row.

Prescriptive teaching strategy 128:

For older children, the teacher prepares a series of directions for a game or project. The child has to repeat the sequence and try to play the game or make the required object.

Auditory Sequential Memory: the ability to remember the correct order of auditorily presented material.

Remedial Objective: to help the student develop skills in the recall of serially presented auditory material.

Prescriptive teaching strategy 129:

Instruct the child to listen while the teacher taps out a pattern with her pencil. Require the child to repeat it. Similar patterns may be made by clapping hands or tapping feet.

Prescriptive teaching strategy 130:

Ask the child to listen to a series of numbers and then request that he name selected ones such as the fourth one, the largest one, the middle one and so on.

Prescriptive teaching strategy 131:

The teacher presents a series of related common items, for example, four vegetables. The child is asked to repeat the series in the exact order in which it was presented.

Prescriptive teaching strategy 132:

The teacher begins a game by saying, "Today, I am going to pack my suitcase and I am putting in my shoes." The game continues with each child adding something to the suitcase, while remembering in the correct sequence the previous items.

Prescriptive teaching strategy 133:

The teacher tells the student a story. The child is then given an unordered list of the events from the story. The child's task is to rearrange the events in their proper sequence.

Auditory Decoding: the ability to derive meaning from auditorily presented material.

Remedial Objective: to help the child develop skills involving the integration of various components of auditory perception.

Prescriptive teaching strategy 134:

The child is required to respond when instructed by the teacher to hop, skip or jump a designated number of times. Presumably the selected activities are familiar to the student and the teacher need not demonstrate.

Prescriptive teaching strategy 135:

The teacher directs the children to reach for the sky when a high note is played by a musical instrument and to touch the floor when a low note is sounded.

Prescriptive teaching strategy 136:

The teacher verbally presents a variety of words with selected initial sounds *fox, church, egg).* After the presentation of each word a child is directed to look around the room and find five things that begin with the same sounds.

Prescriptive teaching strategy 137:

The child is asked to draw a picture with the teacher's guidance. For example, "At the top of your page, draw a yellow moon. At the bottom on the right draw a big pumpkin and a smaller one next to it. Draw a scarecrow in the middle of the page. Draw three small black cats sitting in the grass to the left of the scarecrow. Draw a straw hat on the scarecrow." The children are told that the directions will be given only once and that they must listen carefully.

Prescriptive teaching strategy 138:

Using books from the curriculum, ask the children to locate certain words or objects in response to the teacher's directions. For example, "Tell me the sixth word in the tenth sentence on page four."

6/ Haptic Perception

The importance of touch and adequate cutaneous stimulation in infant learning has been discussed by Montagu (1971) in his book *Touching: The Human Significance of the Skin*. He claims that the sequence of sensory development in the infant is tactile—auditory—visual. In his 1962 title, Montagu refers to the work of Hooker to illustrate the early development of the tactile modality:

> External pressure applied to the fetus through the mother's abdominal wall will elicit increasing activity with the age of the fetus. Davenport Hooker and others have shown that the human fetus becomes reflexly capable of responding to tactile stimulation at seven- and- a half weeks. Direct stimulation of the human fetus removed from the uterus is most immediately responded to in the mouth-nose area. Stimulated with a horse-hair bristle in the facial region such a very young fetus will respond with bending of the neck and side usually in the direction opposite that of the stimulated side, accompanied by some backward movement of both arms at the shoulder, by a slight rotation of the pelvic regions and very slight abduction of the thighs. As the fetus grows his movements become more vigorous and sharply defined; so that pressure upon his body from outside will tend to elicit increasingly more vigorous responses as he grows older.

Emphasis is given by Montagu to early tactile and auditory stimulation and its significance for later visual dominance in the child. The processes of feeling and hearing provide a more meaningful visual experience than vision alone.

Various authors in Solomon's (1965) book entitled *Sensory Deprivation* conclude that man's cognitive and emotional functions are affected by deprivation of normal tactile, visual, auditory, and proprioceptive experiences. Casler (1965) states that functioning on the Gesell schedule can be improved in institutionalized infants by giving additional tactile stimulation. Ayres (1964) has found that tactile deficits are common among hyperactive and distractible children. She reports that tactile stimualtion improves tactile perception, and also suggests that cutaneous stimulation experiences should be provided prior to any perceptual-motor training.

Increased awarness of the tactile-kinesthetic modalities seems to be a prerequisite to the improvement of skills in interpersonal and academic activities. It would seem logical, therefore, to incorporate these sensory modalities into a learning paradigm for both the 3R curriculum *and* social adjustment education.

An example of an occasion in which the tactile-kinesthetic senses are significant to interpersonal relations is the handshake. A long vigorous handshake conveys a very different meaning than one that is brief and limp. An article by Herbert A. Otto in *Ways of Growth: Approaches to Expanding Human Awareness* (1968) and Ronald Levy's (1973) chapter "Magic of Touch" provide a very readable account of the use of the tactile-kinesthetic senses in developing human awareness. The second volume of the 1970 "Practical Handbook" series by Pfeiffer and Jones outlines a number of nonverbal techniques which can be used to enhance and supplement social learning that is the result of verbal interaction. Illustrations of the use of the tactile-kinesthetic modalities in teaching basic school subjects are included in the subsequent discussion of remedial approaches which employ these two modalities in their procedures.

The tactile-kinesthetic modalities are often neglected in the remediation of learning disabilities in reading, writing and spelling. This is especially difficult to understand because three of the major remedial approaches using these modalities were formulated and implemented prior to 1945. The references which describe these three procedures are:

> The early work of Maria Montessori; the translation to English of *The Montessori Method* and *Dr. Montessori's Own Handbook* appeared in 1912 and 1914 respectively;
> Grace Fernald's *Remedial Techniques in Basic School Subjects*, originally published in 1943;
> Anna Gillingham and Bessie Stillman's 1946 *Remedial Training for Children With Specific Disabilities in Reading, Spelling, and Pennmanship*.

All of these titles are still in print: the latest printing of *Dr. Montessori's Own Handbook* was in 1967; Fernald's handbook in 1971; the seventh edition of Gillingham-Stillman's book in 1968, and *The Montessori Method* in 1965. An examination of these three approaches and a fourth by Harriet and Harold Blau (1969) will be preceded by a discussion of tactile-kinesthetic perception, the function of which will be threefold:

1. To describe the tactile-kinesthetic modalities;
2. To study tactile and kinesthetic dysfunctions;
3. To examine the role of these two modalities in remediating deficits in basic school subjects.

According to Lerner (1971), "information received through two modalities—tactile and kinesthetic" is referred to as haptic perception. Haptic stimuli provide the learner with one of the three main sources of information about the environment—the others being visual and auditory stimuli. *Tactile perception* refers to information obtained "via the fingers and skin surfaces" (Lerner, 1971) which may provide more distinct impressions than that provided through vision (Fieandt, cited in Barraga, 1976). Gibson (1966) states in *The Senses Considered as Perceptual Systems* that external stimuli contacting the skin activate the tactile sense via receptors in the skin and underlying tissue. Cutaneous stimulation is a composite of the following subsystems:

1. Cutaneous touch: awareness of objects contacting and exerting pressure on the skin;
2. Touch temperature: awareness of the temperature of objects which come into contact with the skin;
3. Touch pain: awareness and registration of pain.

The information received through the tactile modality includes geometric information concerning angle, shape and size; knowledge of surface texture such as "roughness" or "smoothness"; the qualities of "softness" and "hardness"; pressure and temperature (Chalfant and Scheffelin, 1969).

The second component of the haptic process—*kinesthetic perception*—involves information "obtained through body movements and muscle feeling" (Lerner, 1971). According to this definition, the awareness of different parts of the body, and feelings of muscular contraction and relaxation are examples of kinesthetic perception. Wallace and McLoughlin (1975) also equate kinesthetic perception with the "sense of bodily movements" and note that children with disturbances in kinesthetic perception may have problems with coordination, body image and spatial orientation. Hallahan and Kauffman (1976) define the kinesthetic modality as "those bodily sensations gained when one moves." It follows from this definition that different sensations are received when different body parts are moved or when the same body part is moved in different ways. The relevance of kinesthetic perception to teaching the learning disabled child is cited by Barraga (1976): "Using the muscles kinesthetically in movement or in handling materials gives the most comprehensive and precise information."

Activation of the kinesthetic system is initiated by skeletal or muscular movement (Gibson, 1966) and includes:

1. Awareness through joint receptors of the movement and position of the limbs;
2. Awareness of muscular movement by means of receptors which provide feedback concerning, for example, contrasting movements, such as clinching the fist and relaxing the hand. The feedback from both the *muscle receptors and joint receptors* constitute kinesthetic awareness of bodily movements in many activities;
3. Feedback from the inner ear about the position of the head relative to the ground.

Kinesthetic receptors are found in the muscles, tendons, joints, blood vessels, and in the hair cells of the inner ear. In contrast to the environmental information provided by the tactile sense, the kinesthetic modality provides information concerning the body. This information includes limb position, movement patterns of the trunk, arms and legs, and sensitivity to direction of movement, such as backward, forward, up and down.

Methods employing the haptic modality do not appear to assess the child's adeptness in tactile or kinesthetic activities prior to prescribing remedial activities for difficulties in reading and writing. In view of this, it may be advisable to administer Ayres's *Southern California Sensory Integration Tests* and the *Purdue Perceptual-Motor Survey* to assess the child's tactile and kinesthetic skills before employing these teaching strategies. It is not known whether children with deficiencies in either or both of the haptic channels will benefit from activities used in multisensory remedial approaches. The authors of this handbook suggest that if a deficit were suspected, activities such as those described in the remedial section of this chapter might be used to improve the child's performance.

If the child does not have difficulties in the tactile-kinesthetic modalities, we might use one of the following multisensory approaches geared to remediation of learning deficits in the visual or auditory channels:

1. The VAKT multisensory method of Fernald;
2. The AKT approach of Harold and Harriet Blau;
3. Gillingham and Stillman's method;
4. Montessori's tactile-kinesthetic approach.

VAKT Method

Although the purpose of the VAKT method (Visual-Auditory- Kinesthetic-Tactile) is not to develop tactile and kinesthetic skills, it uses these two modalities in conjunction with vision and audition to present a multisensory approach to the teaching of reading and writing. Perception of the unit of meaning—the word—is basic to the method and is maintained by observing the following three guidelines: First, the words to be learned are written for the child in large blackboard-size cursive writing. Writing tends to help the child "see and feel" the word as a single unit rather than as a separate group of letters. Second, erasures are not permitted since Fernald believes that erasing and correcting single letters or syllables breaks the word into meaningless units. If the child does make a mistake he must begin the word anew. Third, after tracing the word several times, the child should write it without looking at the copy. Looking back and forth while writing the word tends to break the unity of the word. The eye movement training which results from seeing words rather than individual letters later assists the child in reading to perceive meaningful word groups rather than individual words (Fernald, 1943).

In the VAKT technique, the story and the words are selected by the student. Because of these characteristics, would it be possible to describe Fernald's word-learning technique as having a cognitive component? Hammill and Bartel (1975) would appear to agree. These writers refer to the Fernald word-learning technique as a "cognitive approach" because "the words originate with the reader and have contextual and meaningful association." The words that the child does not know are written for him in large blackboard-size cursive writing by the teacher. The teacher also explains the meaning of any words used by the child which appear to be unfamiliar to him.

Although word unity is inherent in the procedure, it nonetheless emphasizes *syllabication.* How is it possible to maintain the word as the basic unit of remediation and at the same time incorporate the procedure of syllabication? This question is perhaps best answered by making specific reference to the syllabication procedure and its rationale as originally presented by Fernald. The child must say each part of the word either to himself or aloud as he traces it and as he writes it. This is necessary to establish the connection between the sound of the word and its written form so that the individual will eventually recognize the word from the visual stimulus alone. Fernald (1943) cautions, in accordance with this procedure, that:

> It is important that this vocalization of the word be natural; that is, it should be a repetition of the word as it actually sounds, and not a stilted, distorted sounding out of letters or syllables in such a way that the word is lost in the process. The word *must* is said as it sounds and not mouthed over with the *m* drawn out to *mu,* then the *u,* then the *s* hissed through, and finally the *t* clicked over and drawn out. The sound for each letter is never given separately nor over-emphasized. In a longer word like *important,* the child says the *im* while he is

tracing the first syllable, and *tant* as he traces the last syllable. In writing the word he again pronounces each syllable as he writes it.

The uniqueness of the Fernald word-tracing method has been postulated by Miller (1973) to be the reason for its success. The method is unique because it emphasizes left to right progression, syllabication, and reading for meaning.

A number of criticisms have been directed against the Fernald word-tracing technique by several writers of recent texts in learning disabilities (Hammill and Bartel, 1975; Gearheart, 1976; Gearheart, 1977). These criticisms are listed in point form:

1. The VAKT approach is basically a word-learning technique and does not provide the child with skills in reading comprehension;
2. Children who have at least two years of schooling and who have been thoroughly exposed to reading will benefit most from the simultaneous VAKT strategy. It is not likely to be effective with those who have had little experience in school;
3. Because the effectiveness of the word-tracing method depends on the ability to accurately receive kinesthetic and tactile information, it may have reduced effectiveness with students showing poor performance in activities requiring the use of these sensory modalities;
4. Certain types of neurological dysfunction may cause an overloading of the receptive mechanisms if too many signals are received simultaneously. Although not an established fact, it is possible that this may occur when dealing with hyperactive children. With reference to this criticism, Cruickshank's *A Teaching Method for Brain-Injured and Hyperactive Children* (1961) provides suggestions for reducing stimuli in the classroom which might distract the child and interfere with his learning, for example, opaque windows, identical colour of walls, woodwork and furniture, removal of bulletin boards and pencil sharpeners, etc.

The review articles by Zentall (1975; 1977) suggest that there is more support for educational strategies involving increased stimulation than for those that employ stimulus reduction. Stimulant medication prescribed for hyperactive behaviour, for example, usually brings about an unexpected decrease in distractible behaviours and an increased attention span. Increased novelty incorporated into the learning task and increased movement at a distal location in the classroom (e.g., fish moving about in an aquarium) also have been found to reduce hyperactive and distractible behaviours.

Consistent with the optimum stimulation model, the authors

suggest that the four tactile-kinesthetic educational therapies may work especially well with young children showing hyperactive behaviour because of the increased novelty or *increased stimulation* inherent in the procedures. The novelty of the remedial procedures may help a child to ignore irrelevant stimuli and to attend to the learning task.

AKT Method

In accordance with the caution against sensory overloading, Harold and Harriet Blau (1969) have proposed a multisensory approach based on the assumption that the visual channel may be interfering with the auditory, kinesthetic and tactile modalities. They do not recommend inclusion of visual stimuli in the initial stages of remediation. Their approach is a *nonvisual* one involving the simultaneous use of the auditory, kinesthetic and tactile modalities. Although not included by the Blaus in the rationale for their procedure, the word is still basic to the procedure as in the Fernald method.

The following steps describe their AKT method:

1. To eliminate the visual input, the child is either blindfolded or asked to close his eyes. Whereas in the Fernald approach the function of the tactile-kinesthetic input is to *strengthen* the visual processing of information, the AKT Blau strategy stresses the necessity of *eliminating visual input,* at least in the initial stages of remediation, to increase the effectiveness of the other three modalities;
2. The teacher traces a *word* on the child's back. It is not specified whether the word is traced in writing or printing, which leads to the assumption that there is no preference for either the written or printed form of the word;
3. As the teacher traces the word, letter by letter, on the child's back, she spells it aloud. This point in the procedure marks the introduction of the auditory component;
4. While the teacher traces the word on the student's back, the child, still blindfolded, uses his fingertips to trace the word placed in front of him in *three-dimensional letters.* At this stage the child is involved in using the kinesthetic-tactile modalities. Step four is included unless the teacher suspects that it will either overload the sensory channels or be "too advanced" for the child. The Blaus do not amplify how to determine if sensory overloading will occur nor define "too advanced." Regardless of whether or not step four is included, the next step in the progression is to step five;

5. The child has to reproduce the proper sequence of letters from a scramble of three-dimensional letters;
6. When the child has correctly arranged the letters, he opens his eyes or removes the blindfold, and *visually* experiences the letter sequence or word. Isolation of the visual sense from the auditory, kinesthetic and tactile channels, rather than its use in conjunction with these modalities, is evident here. The interference of vision with these other modalities is presumably eliminated because the only modality operating in this phase is vision. The child is *not touching* the letters (tactile modality), is *not tracing* them (kinesthetic-tactile modality), and is *not hearing* the individual letters of the word being spelled aloud by either the teacher or himself (auditory modality);
7. As a concluding step, the pupil is required to write the word and to file it for "future review." The child plays a somewhat passive role in the first three phases of the approach, whereas he is involved in a more active-expressive role in steps four to seven.

There is one point of caution concerning the use of the haptic sense in remedial activities. This concern is not related to distractible behaviour but to tactile defensiveness. There is evidence that distractible and hyperactive children tend to react defensively to being touched or to the anticipation of being touched (Ayres, 1964; Bauer, 1977). Tactile defensiveness is often manifested in complaints, increased movement, physical withdrawal of body parts and even somatic complaints and excuses to discontinue the tactile-kinesthetic activity. It follows that these tactile defensive behaviours may interfere with the remedial activity and consequently the child may receive little benefit from educational strategies employing the haptic sense. Tactile defensiveness may be exacerbated in the initial stages of the Blau and Blau procedure since the child cannot see where he is being touched.

Gillingham and Stillman

In contrast to teaching a child to recognize whole words by sight, the objective of the word-building method of Gillingham and Stillman (1968) is to first teach letter sounds and then to combine these letter sounds into words. This technique which they describe in the context of their "learning triangle" depends on the close association of the visual, auditory and kinesthetic modalities.

Gillingham and Stillman claim that involving the tactile-kinesthetic senses in the tracing of the letters is "the best if not the only means" of teaching memory for form. Visual exposure to the letter may not be sufficient for the child to remember its correct printed or written form.

Memory for the letter is strengthened when the kinesthetic movement is used in tracing the letter. Tracing, according to these writers, should be accompanied by appropriate verbal instructions for making each letter.

As in the Fernald method, cursive writing rather than printing is recommended, although the Gillingham-Stillman rationale is quite different. The function of writing in the VAKT procedures is to maintain the visual unity of the word, whereas in the Gillingham-Stillman technique it is to *reduce the number of easily reversed letters* and hence the possibility of the child making reversals. For example, some letters are more similar in printed form (b and d) than in written form (*ℓ* and *d*) and, therefore, may be more easily reversed by the child.

In applying their multisensory approach to spelling, these writers recommend a four-point strategy. After the student hears the teacher say a word, he immediately repeats it. This word repetition not only accentuates the auditory component of learning but allows the child to kinesthetically experience the movements involved in the vocalization of the word. The teacher then *names the letters* of the word in proper sequence, after which the student names them. Showing the word to the child after it has been auditorily and kinesthetically experienced introduces the visual channel to the learning sequence. As a final step, visual memory for the letters is reinforced by requiring the student to *trace the individual letters* and to spell the word aloud as he traces. This is frequently referred to by Gillingham and Stillman as the *Simultaneous-Oral-Spelling Technique*. Although the technique involves both oral and written spelling, more emphasis is given by the writers to the oral component, as reflected in the name given to this technique. This technique cannot be easily applied to nonphonetic words, such as "cough" and "laugh," which are not spelled as pronounced. In learning to spell this type of word, they recommend auditory and kinesthetic remedial activities, especially for children with poor visual memory. While the child with poor visual memory is tracing the word letter by letter, it is essential that the teacher distinctly pronounce each letter sound, that the child immediately echo the letter sound said by the teacher, and that this auditory sequence be immediately followed by naming the letter.

Although not specifically stated by Gillingham and Stillman, two points come to mind concerning their procedure. First, the kinesthetic movement involved in letter tracing seems to play a more dominant role than the associated tactile component. In fact, there is no reference to either the role or possible effectiveness of the tactile sense in learning to spell. Second, by stating that the learner's eyes be averted from the letter to focus attention on feeling the form, Gillingham and Stillman suggest that vision interferes with or reduces the efficiency of the auditory and kinesthetic channels. Note the similarity to the visual reduction technique of Blau and Blau.

Montessori's Method

Montessori (1914) stresses that training in gross tactile-kinesthetic discrimination should precede the use of these modalities for letter discrimination, with activities structured so that the child experiences only success. Initially he practises touching contrasting surfaces, such as coarse and fine sandpaper, with his fingertips, followed by lightly touching a number of cloth samples of various textures and, finally, matching cloth samples of identical texture by *touching* and *feeling* them. Following training in discriminating surface texture, exercises for gross shape discrimination are introduced. Beginning with very different geometrical figures, such as a circle, a square and a triangle, the child is required to place them in the appropriate position in a formboard. Montessori maintains that *control of error* is inherent in the procedure because a figure cannot be inserted into the formboard unless it is placed in the form that corresponds exactly with its shape. With his index and middle fingers, the child is also directed to touch the outline of the geometrical inserts as well as the shapes in the formboard.

According to Montessori (1912), there are two kinesthetic components requisite to writing:

1. The movement necessary for forming the letters;
2. Correctly holding and manipulation of the pencil.

Skill in performing the kinesthetic movement involved in writing is acquired by tracing letters "in the fashion of flowing writing" which establishes a motor memory for the task. Since the child is required "to follow the visual image of the outlined letter," this tactile-kinesthetic movement reinforces the visual image for the letters.

The transition from letter tracing to holding and manipulating the pencil is facilitated by tracing with the fingers that are involved in holding the pencil, that is, the index and middle fingers. The student at this stage should be familiar with using these two fingers for tracing as a result of his prior experience in activities for developing gross tactile-kinesthetic discrimination. Further preparation for the acquisition of the coordination required to hold and manipulate the pencil involves specific exercises in which he actually uses a pencil. To develop this skill, the child draws around the contours of geometric figures and, after removing the figures, proceeds to fill them in, holding the pencil as he would in writing. Gradually, the haphazard lines become "longer and more nearly parallel" and more coordination is shown as fewer and fewer lines extend outside the boundaries of the figures.

Although it seems that the tactile sense has been assigned a lesser role than the kinesthetic, Montessori does indeed recommend its inclusion in writing activities. This is evident in the use of sandpaper letters for tracing. The importance of the visual channel is also apparent in the system of using colour-coded sandpaper letters: vowels in light-coloured sandpaper mounted on dark cards, and consonants in black sandpaper affixed to white cards.

After the student has received training in the prerequisite kinesthetic activities of *tracing* the letters and *manipulating* the pencil, specific procedures for recognizing and writing vowels and consonants are introduced in a series of steps. The teacher gives a sandpaper letter to the child, names the letter, and enunciates its sound. When the child hears the sound, he associates it with the visual image of the letter. Guided by the rough surface of the sandpaper, and with eyes open, the student *traces* the letter with his index and middle fingers. If necessary, the child's index finger is guided so that the tracing is done from left to right as in writing. As soon as the child hears the sound of the letter and begins to trace, he simultaneously associates the visual image of the letter with its tactile-kinesthetic impression. These steps should be repeated until the child knows the association between the sound and the letter. The student is alerted by his tactile sense to any error he may make because of the contrast between the sandpaper letter and its smooth background. This immediate feedback is another illustration of the control of error inherent in Montessori's methods.

Montessori has incorporated an assessment procedure into her remedial strategy to determine if the child has learned the association between the sound of the letter and its visual form. The following sample item illustrates the type of questions included in this assessment period:

"Show me the letter that makes the /m/ sound."

The pupil chooses from each pair of letters presented to him the one that corresponds to the letter sound enunciated by the teacher. If he does not recognize the letters by visually inspecting them, the tracing procedure is repeated. When the child can match the sound of a letter with its written form, he is then asked to give the *names* of letters which are presented individually in written form. For example, if the letter *m* were presented and the child were asked, "What is this letter?" he should respond with the appropriate name of the letter. If he cannot name the letter, additional training in sound-letter association is recommended.

Additional guidelines are provided by Montessori for the teaching of consonants. At least two or three vowels should be taught before consonants are introduced. Her rationale for this is that once the child knows two or three vowels, he can then be exposed to simple words or blends of sounds which are combinations of these vowels with a few or even one consonant. The teacher first pronounces the *sound* of the consonant several times by itself (/m/,/m/,/m/), combines it with a vowel and pronounces this syllable or word (/me/,/me/,/me/), and again pronounces just the sound of the consonant (/m/,/m/,/m/). When the child has learned a few more vowels and consonants, he can be introduced to longer words. The letters that he knows are placed in front of him, and after the teacher says a word, e.g., *papa*, distinctly pronouncing the *p* a number of times, the child is asked to select the letter that corresponds to the /p/ sound. Subsequent letters of the word are similarly selected by the child with the teacher repeating the word several times, emphasizing the sound of the letter to be selected. Because the second syllable in this example is a repetition of the first, the child can readily compose it. The pupil places each letter one after the other and in this manner each new word is composed.

After completing this procedure, Montessori believes that the child has the skills necessary "to read any word; that is, he knows how to read the sounds which compose it." She also believes that by using her method the child is *simultaneously* taught to read and write. The rationale is this: when the child "sees and recognizes" vowels and consonants "he reads, and when he traces he writes."

In conclusion, a number of contrasts between Montessori's procedures and the VAKT technique of Fernald should be noted. The *word* is the basic unit of instruction in the Fernald method, whereas Montessori begins remediation with individual letters and progresses to words. The original purpose of Montessori's approach was not primarily to remediate but to teach young children with little or no experience in school. Her method, therefore, may be used in developing readiness skills as well as in remediating learning problems.

Preference for the various modalities in remedial strategies varies, suggesting that more research is needed before it can be determined whether vision, active touch, or a combination of both is the most effective mode of learning. Although vision has been found by some researchers (Raskin and Baker, 1975) to be the superior modality, others such as Montagu (1971) and Ayres (1964) stress the importance of the tactile and kinesthetic senses in learning. Remedial teaching specialists such as Montessori and Blau and Blau also assign more importance to the tactile-kinesthetic modalities. Since the major remedial teaching strategies differ with regard to their preferences for certain modalities, and since research is not yet conclusive as to which is more effective, the authors suggest the following guidelines to assist the remedial teacher in selecting an appropriate teaching strategy. Visual presentation of letters, shapes, numbers, etc., should be provided for the child. If he experiences difficulty with the visual material, both tactile and visual information can be presented simultaneously. The rationale for this sequence (Raskin and Baker, 1975) is that if cross-modal transfer occurs in learning, it will be best accomplished when a visual task is introduced before a tactile task. Other modalities may be added to the teaching procedure until it is determined which approach is the most effective for a particular child.

It may seem that the remedial activities prescribed by Fernald, Blau and Blau, Gillingham, Stillman, and Montessori are more appropriate to the "remedial activities" section of this chapter. The rationale for their inclusion in the theory aspect is that the nature and detail of these activities warrants a more theoretical discussion than would be permitted within the format of the "remedial activities" section.

The remedial activities that immediately follow in this chapter are activities to improve the child's skills in tactile-kinesthetic tasks. A number of these activities should be used prior to employing any of the remedial strategies that have been discussed. They may also serve as test items in assessing the child's competence in tactile-kinesthetic skills.

Suggested Strategies

Tactile-kinesthetic awareness: the ability to explore information concerning one's environment through a finger movement procedure.

Remedial Objective: to facilitate learning skills involving finger movements, touch and muscle feedback.

Prescriptive teaching strategy 139:

Present the child with some wet objects, such as sand, mud and a sponge. Ask the child to feel each of the objects until he understands the concept "wet." Present him with the same objects in their dry form. He might then be asked to sort a variety of unseen objects into wet and dry categories.

Prescriptive teaching strategy 140:

Present the child with different kinds of fruit and let him examine the texture of each as well as its shape and size. Blindfold the child and place each of the objects in turn in his hands. The child is requested to describe how each fruit feels and attempt to identify it.

Prescriptive teaching strategy 141:

As an extension of strategy 140 give the child a piece of cotton wool, and a wooden block and ask hin to describe how each feels until he recognizes the differences between "soft" and "hard."

Haptic discrimination: the ability to distinguish between objects by touch and movement.

Remedial Objective: to facilitate skill in using the fingertips to detect physical differences between stimuli.

Prescriptive teaching strategy 142:

Instruct the child to touch common objects—play furniture, toys and games. As a second step the objects are covered and the child has to find each upon request through touch. Initially both hands may be used; next, the dominant hand, and finally the nondominant hand.

Prescriptive teaching strategy 143:

Place a button in the child's hand and let him become thoroughly familiar with it by manipulating it. Blindfold the child and hide the buttom among a group of small objects and ask the child to find it.

Prescriptive teaching strategy 144:

Take several sheets of different sandpaper grits and have the child describe how they feel and arrange them from "smooth" to "very rough." Then, have him place his hands behind his back while the teacher rubs the selected sandpaper samples over his palm. The student tries to identify which grit of sandpaper has been used.

Prescriptive teaching strategy 145:

With glue, draw a number or letter on a piece of cardboard. Sprinkle sand over the glue and let it dry. Present the cards to the child while he has his eyes closed and let him feel the number or letter, and try to name it. A subsequent activity would be to request the child to draw the number or letter that he has just traced with his fingers.

Prescriptive teaching strategy 146:

An interesting addition to strategy 145 would be to design letters or numbers on cardboard by using a paper punch. The child attempts to identify the figures by touch.

Prescriptive teaching strategy 147:

The teacher selects a group of objects which range in weight from light to heavy. There should be a noticeable difference in weight between the successive objects. Have the child arrange the objects in serial order from light to heavy.

Prescriptive teaching strategy 148:

As an extension of strategy 147 the child could be required to match the objects with a set of objects of identical weight presented by the teacher.

Prescriptive teaching strategy 149:

Ask the child to describe some of the things he experienced while walking to school such as "wind on his face," "warmth of the sun," "coldness of the snow."

Prescriptive teaching strategy 150:

After experience in kinesthetic awareness activities, ask each child in the class to design a poster affixing *materials* belonging to different categories. If actual materials or objects are not available, magazine or catalogue cutouts might serve as a substitute activity. The posters could be displayed in the classroom as a shared activity.

7/Mathematical Disorders

Learning problems associated with mathematics are many. To suggest that one chapter in a handbook such as this could encompass either diagnosis or remediation in toto would be ludicrous. Given the complexity of the area and the synthesis of perceptual and cognitive skills required to perform adequately in mathematics, it would be a travesty to think of it as simplistic or easily explained.

These considerations notwithstanding, this chapter will focus upon a few common problematic areas. The authors realize that the ensuing suggestions represent a finger in the dike rather than a careful and all encompassing methical approach to learning problems in the area of mathematics.

The exact stages in the evolution of mathematics, or for that matter numbers, are not really known. It has been suggested that early man possessed *number sense*, long before there was a formalized concept of counting (Dantzig, 1939). For example, members of early civilizations used a system to identify animals by relating a pebble to each. By establishing a one-to-one correspondence between animals and pebbles, they were actually applying a primitive form of counting.

Johnson and Myklebust (1967) suggest that a similar sequence can be observed in the ontogenetic development of number concepts in children. That is, children do not suddenly at school age acquire an understanding of arithmetic solely through exposure to instruction. Also, children who at the age of four can count to ten are not necessarily displaying a special aptitude for math.

Instead, children acquire through their environment the basic concepts which are prerequisite to the acquisition of more advanced number concepts. The child who stands under the kitchen table, and then bumps his head when he tries to stand up under an end table is learning the "higher-lower" concept. Similarly *too much, all gone, all done, more* and so on are learned through home experience. Through such experience children acquire an information bank which eventually becomes the source of mental perception and the understanding of number symbols (Gesell and Amatruda, 1947).

Piaget, Montessori and others have indicated that basic number concepts develop spontaneously through the child's interaction with his environment. By seeing, touching, saying and manipulating he learns to count on his fingers and acquire basic concepts, such as one-to-one correspondence. Piaget (1953) stated that it is erroneous to suppose that children acquire the concept of numbers simply from instruction, not just from teaching, warning that when adults try to impose mathematical concepts on a child too early the learning which results is verbal pseudo-learning.

It is a well-established fact that each year a limited number of children (possibly somewhat less than 5 per cent) enter the school system destined to have problems in mathematics. The reasons for such failure range from developmental lag to organic impairment. Included in the list of causes for failure in mathematics are such things as limited intellectual capacity, poor motivation and inadequate teaching. A distinction is usually made between such problems and those of a more specific nature relating to neurological functioning. Much research has been conducted in an attempt to relate specific problems to etiological factors—injury in the womb, meningitis, parietal lobe lesion. Based upon research in mathematical disorders, various researchers have chosen to label disabilities with number and calculation *acalculia* (if there is a complete loss) and *dyscalculia* (if partial). Cohn (1968) described dyscalculia as "failure to recognize or manipulate number symbols in an advanced culture." Rather than frame our discussion in such terms, we shall approach such disorders, for the most part, from a classroom perspective.

Often it is not until the child is confronted with arithmetic in the primary grades that a deficit becomes evident. This was more a problem in past years when a larger part of arithmetic consisted of rote learning. According to Squires (1976) this is not so much the case today in that modern mathematics programs place more emphasis on individual discovery. Modern math, or the so-called "new math," makes it possible to identify a child with a disability related to number symbols much earlier in his school experience. This, coupled with a growing awareness of specific learning disabilities, has helped to expose those who cannot cope with mathematics for reasons other than general mental retardation, sensory handicaps, poor preparation, or inadequate instruction.

Johnson and Myklebust (1967) make a distinction between children who fail in arithmetic because of language and reading problems which are not confined to arithmetic and those who have disturbances in quantitative thinking. Making the same distinction, Kosc (1974) stated that dyscalculia refers "specifically to a disorder of the special abilities for mathematics without a simultaneous defect in general mental abilities."

In the nonspecific class are placed various learning disabilities which, though not specific to the cognitive processes of mathematics, are interfering factors which must be compensated for in any program of instruction. That is to say, a child can experience failure in arithmetic because he cannot revisualize numbers, cannot remember instructions or cannot form written numbers. The list of problems pervasive to learning in general rather than mathematics in particular is infinite—auditory imperception, right-left confusion, body image distortion, perseveration, visual motor difficulty and so on (Silver and Hagin, 1960). These disturbances interfere with arithmetic learning but are not regarded as disturbances in quantitative thinking in the traditional sense. Some disorders of this variety as presented by Johnson and Myklebust are summarized below.

Auditory Receptive Language Disorders

These disorders are demonstrated by the child who has great difficulty understanding the words used to describe certain processes or in grasping word meanings in story problems. To him numbers are more stable than verbal symbols since each number represents a certain quantity and neither the symbol nor its meaning changes. In contrast, spoken words vary in meaning and are problematic.

As noted by Johnson and Myklebust (1967), an auditory receptive disorder can interfere with one's ability in arithmetic because the many words used in describing mathematical processes—set, times, base—become unusually difficult.

Auditory Memory Disorders

Memory problems can interfere with mathematics in various ways. At the most basic level, if a child cannot recall numbers which have been presented he has a problem. In like fashion, if he correctly recognizes numbers when he hears them but cannot hold them in mind long enough to make an appropriate response reading numbers aloud, rapid oral drills and oral calculations will prove to be very frustrating.

Reading Disorders

It is not always the case that reading disorders will seriously impede a child in mathematics; sometimes only the ability to understand story problems suffers. In dealing with numbers, the child with a reading problem does not necessarily encounter similar difficulty since the processing of numerical symbols does not require the high degree of auditory-visual analysis and synthesis characteristic of reading. For example, in reading the word *telephone* the child must decode the sequence of sounds with the letters and then blend them to form the word. With the number 4 there is only one visual symbol related to the word. Difficulty might be anticipated if the word *four* were used instead.

In other cases visual perceptual disorders associated with reading (such as reversals and inversions) present a similar problem with numbers as with letters. In such cases similar remedial suggestions have been successfully utilized. According to Johnson and Myklebust (1967), a child who has trouble revisualizing numbers may require visual cues until the deficiency is corrected, i.e., a clock face where he can see the numbers in proper sequence.

Although Johnson and Myklebust do not consider reading problems per se as dyscalculia, Kosc (1974) has employed the term *lexical dyscalculia* to describe the inability to read mathematical symbols such as digits, numbers, operational signs and written mathematical operations. Often such children interchange similar looking digits (6 for 9) and reverse two digit numbers when reading (13 as 31). Irrespective of the assignment of labels, a reading problem can create a dysfunction in mathematics.

Writing Disorders

Kosc (1974) described writing disorders associated with numbers as *graphical dyscalculia* viewing it as dysgraphia extended into arithmetic. Characteristics of this type of disorder are the tendency to write digits in reverse order, the tendency to ignore zeros (20073 written as 27300 or 20730) and, in more serious cases, the inability to write numbers which have been dictated.

In the most serious situations, Johnson and Myklebust (1967) suggest that the children should not be urged to form the numbers. Instead multiple-choice answers may be used or possibly a rubber stamp set of numbers.

Distinct from learning problems such as those just described, Johnson and Myklebust (1967) point out the existence of *quantitative thinking disturbances* which are indigenous to mathematics and involve the understanding of mathematical principles and processes. They have presented a number of disabilities which may be found in varying degrees among cases of disturbed quantitative thinking:

1. Inability to establish a one-to-one correspondence, e.g., the number of children in a room cannot be related to the number of seats;

2. Inability to count meaningfully, e.g., child may point to first object and say "1," "2," then to the second and say "3," "4," "5."
3. Inability to associate the auditory and visual symbols, e.g., child may see 6 and call it "seven" or 4 and call it "two";
4. Inability to learn both the cardinal and ordinal systems of counting. This may be an example of perseveration in cases where the child has learned with great difficulty the cardinal system and finds it difficult to make the change;
5. Inability to visualize clusters of objects within a larger group; each object in the group must always be counted;
6. Inability to grasp the principle of conservation of quantity;
7. Inability to perform arithmetic operations;
8. Inability to understand the meaning of process signs, e.g., ×, + or ÷, −, = or >, <;
9. Inability to understand the arrangement of numbers on the page, i.e., could confuse 1234 and 4321;
10. Inability to follow and remember the sequence of steps to be used in various mathematical operations;
11. Inability to understand the principles of measurement;
12. Inability to read maps and graphs;
13. Inability to choose the principles for solving problems in arithmetic reasoning (Johnson and Myklebust, 1967).*

As conceded earlier, this chapter is limited to a cursory look at problems in mathematics. Consequently, the remainder of this discussion and the ensuing strategies will focus upon four areas which are among the most problematic—basic number concept, arithmetic processes, classification and mathematical reasoning.

Number Concept

Number concept or "number sense" is the ability to relate quantity in a consistent way to the symbols which we have agreed to let represent it—12, 45, 8, 19.

As has been noted earlier, the child begins to develop number concepts as early as the first year of life. Often the first attempts to employ numbers are little more than a chanting process in which the child quickly displays pseudo-knowledge by correctly verbalizing numbers, usually from one to ten. The child must learn to match the symbol 4 with an appropriate grouping of candies before we can say that his knowledge is valid; that is, one-to-one correspondence is the most

---

* D. J. Johnson and H. R. Myklebust, *Learning Disabilities: Educational Principles and Practices*, New York: Grune & Stratton, 1967. Reprinted by permission.

basic meaningful acquisition. Without it, the child is unable to decide how many marbles are needed so that one can be given to *each* player in a game involving six children.

Another key aspect of number concept is sequential position. The concept of more and less is dependent upon the understanding that each number has meaning because of its position. The number *seven* has meaning relative to the fact that it is more than six and one less than eight. Later manipulation of numbers through the processes of addition, subtraction, multiplication and division extend from the solid establishment of number concept.

Friedus (1966) has stated that the symbols of mathematical language have to be based upon concrete experience. Similarly Lerner (1976) posits that "the ability to count, to understand one-to-one correspondence, to match, to sort and to compare are dependent upon the child's experience in manipulating objects." When children come to school with experiential deficits in this area, concrete materials can often be provided by the teacher to help facilitate numerical thinking.

Arithmetic Operations

Arithmetic operations depend upon an adequate comprehension of number structure. That is, basic computational skills cannot be completed with speed or accuracy unless the child has thoroughly grasped the underlying knowledge concerning numbers. Once again the teacher is asked to note that rote learning devoid of meaning, similar to "chanting" the alphabet or numbers from one to twenty, can disguise a problem in computation. To be specific, a child may satisfactorily parrot times tables but not be able to apply the principle of multiplication when confronted with six rows of jelly beans each containing seven beans. He may revert to counting rather than applying the appropriate times table.

Although some authors include fractions, decimals and percentages in their discussion of arithmetic operations, the present authors have defined basic computational skills as addition, subtraction, multiplication and division.

Johnson and Myklebust (1967) have presented a number of problems related to arithmetic computation which are worth noting. In some cases the deficit might relate to gaps in knowledge concerning basic numbers or in the reasoning process per se. In other cases confusion is related to a perceptual disturbance such as the inability to visually discriminate between signs: $>$, $<$, $-$, $=$, $\div$, $+$ and $\times$. If the child fails to perceive differences between these symbols, or confuses them with regard to meaning, problems are predictable. Also, left-right confusion and other visual-spatial problems cannot help but interfere.

Memory problems as well can disrupt the performance of mathematical operations. If the child cannot remember and follow the sequence of steps required to divide or multiply, the correct answer will evade him.

Bereiter (cited in Lerner, 1976) has provided guidelines for teaching arithmetic which seem appropriate to our discussion of arithmetic operations. The authors have decided to include these for consideration.

1. The emphasis in arithmetic instruction should be on *finding out* answers to questions, rather than toward merely doing something;
2. Whatever is learned should be *generalized* to many different kinds of applications and experiences with different ways of handling the problem;
3. Beginning mathematics should be made *coherent*, instead of a collection of unrelated topics and tricks (as is sometimes true of modern math instruction);
4. Instruction must be *thorough* so that children have the needed practice. In some modern math programs insufficient time is devoted to practice;
5. The mathematics program should be taught so that the child gains *confidence* in mathematics ability. Adults often become alarmed and defensive when faced with a mathematical problem because they lost confidence during their early arithmetic instruction.

Classification

Classification may be considered part of mathematical reasoning and its treatment as a separate though related entity in this review might be viewed by some as a false dichotomy. Nevertheless, for the sake of clarity, we will define classification as the ability to note likes and differences between objects and to group or categorize them appropriately. The ability to classify seems a natural culmination to the child's early attempts to superimpose order upon his surroundings. In the educational context it is regarded as essential to problem solving and mathematical reasoning.

To properly classify objects the child must be able to consider objects in light of their individual detail while at the same time perceiving points of commonality. To do this the child must overcome the tendency to fixate on less relevant details and systematically organize his perception. In the course of development it is the usual case that perception becomes less egocentric. At the same time, as the child matures, a logical classification system is required. When such milestones are not reached during the course of ontogenetic development, the ability to classify and form concepts suffers. If he is unable to look past detail and generalize from his percepts, his world does not take on the organization and meaning characteristic of mature perception and thought.

The teacher can help to facilitate the child's ability to classify (some may consider classification as tantamount to concept formation) by providing tasks involving sorting, sequencing and comparing objects in terms of their function. It goes almost without saying that concrete experiences are in order as the child first approaches classification.

Mathematical Reasoning

Findings from neurological investigations suggest the existence of special dispositions for mathematics. Although much has been written concerning congenital physiological bases for mathematic problems, Kosc (1974) points out that even good equipment can be impaired during the course of development causing irreparable disorders of mathematical reasoning abilities.

In a general sense mathematical abilities may be viewed as qualities requisite to successful performance in mathematics. Verdelin (1958) equated these abilities with comprehension of the nature of mathematical problems, methods and verifications; ability to learn, memorize and reproduce them; and skill in using them to solve problems. Kosc (1974) used the term *ideognostical dyscalculia* to describe a disorder primarily in understanding mathematical ideas and relations. He noted that in the most serious cases a person may be able to read or write numbers but is unable to interpret what he has read or written. That is, the individual knows that 9 = nine and that nine is to be written 9 but has not grasped that 9 or nine is more than eight and is one less than ten.

As pointed out by Kaliski (1962) many children with neurological problems have perceptual problems of one variety or another. As concepts evolve from percepts in the development of thought processes, it is no surprise to learn that perceptually handicapped children have conceptualization problems. Many show erratic features in thinking such as lack of continuity, difficulty in seeing cause-effect relationships, and farfetched reasoning.

In brief, arithmetic reasoning is the ability to *apply* arithmetic processes to problem solving. The child with an arithmetic reasoning problem may display his disability when attempting to understand weights, measures, fractions, coinage equivalents and time applied to practical life situations. Price comparisons and time differentials are often very problematic. The solution to a simple syllogism can be difficult.

All men are mortal.		Mary is shorter than Alice.
Kings are men.	OR	Alice is shorter than Freda.
Are kings mortal?		Is Freda taller than Mary?

Irrespective of cause, the child who finds it difficult to move beyond the concrete will encounter difficulties with mathematical reasoning.

Suggested Strategies

Number Concept: the ability to use one-to-one correspondence in counting.

Remedial Objective: to help the child achieve a basic understanding of numbers from 0 to 100, as a prerequisite to more advanced mathematical concepts.

Prescriptive teaching strategy 151:
Ask the children to reproduce pegboard or bead-string designs through one-to-one matching.

Prescriptive teaching strategy 152:
Have the child perform an action like dropping a block into a container each time he hears a designated sound, i.e., a bell or a clap. This will eventually help the pupil to establish the correspondence between the number of signals and the number of blocks in the container.

Prescriptive teaching strategy 153:
Show the child a particular number, and direct him to count out that number of objects from an assortment of buttons.

Prescriptive teaching strategy 154:
Arrange objects in sets and introduce the concepts of "more" and "less." The complexity of this task is gradually increased until ten or more objects are used. The child has to count sets of objects, and then using one-to-one correspondence he must decide which set has more objects.

Prescriptive teaching strategy 155:

Give the child a piece of cloth which has four buttons sewed on it. In addition, give him pieces of cloth with three, four and five buttonholes. Instruct him to button the buttons until he finds a piece of cloth that matches perfectly. As he becomes better acquainted with the activity, he may be able to find the right number of buttonholes needed by counting, rather than by actually buttoning.

Prescriptive teaching strategy 156:

Arrange in random order boxes numbered from 1 to 10. Supply the child with marbles or chips. The goal is to put the correct number of objects in the required box, for example, two objects in the "2" box.

Prescriptive teaching strategy 157:

The student is provided with a number of matchbox toys. Each toy has a number on it. A sheet of cardboard with numbered squares on it is given to the child. He has to place each numbered toy in the correct square. This helps to establish number sequence.

Prescriptive teaching strategy 158:

Present five balls numbered from 1 to 5. With a minimum of six children formed in a circle, the balls are tossed back and forth. The teacher calls a number, for example 3, and the child who catches the ball numbered 3 has to bounce it on the floor three times. Repeat using another number.

Prescriptive teaching strategy 159:

Ask the learner to prepare a scrapbook for numbers from 1 to 10. Each page is given a number and the child pastes pictures demonstrating each number.

Arithmetic Processes: the basic operations of addition, subtraction, multiplication and division.

Remedial Objective: to teach the computational skills involved in these arithmetic operations.

Addition and Subtraction

Prescriptive teaching strategy 160:

Give the student two wooden blocks with a different number written on each of the six sides. The child tosses the two blocks and when they land, he adds or subtracts the numbers according to instructions.

Prescriptive teaching strategy 161:

The learner is given a number of beads on a string. He separates them into groups along the string to represent equations such as:

$$1 + 5 = 6 \qquad 4 + 2 = 6 \qquad 6 - 4 = 2 \qquad 6 - 1 = 5$$
$$0 + 6 = 6 \qquad 5 + 1 = 6 \qquad 6 - 5 = 1 \qquad 6 - 0 = 6$$
$$3 + 3 = 6 \qquad 2 + 4 = 6 \qquad 6 - 3 = 3 \qquad 6 - 2 = 4$$

Prescriptive teaching strategy 162:

In each section of an egg carton, write an addition or subtraction problem. Two children are each given a marble and are seated at opposite ends of the carton. Each child tosses his marble and must answer the problem which is written in the section where his marble lands.

Prescriptive teaching strategy 163:

The children are given paper flower petals on which are written addition and subtraction questions. The teacher calls out a number and if the child has a petal whose answer equals the presented number he uses it to construct a flower by pasting it on an outline of a six-petal flower. That is, the teacher calls the number 7 and the child responds by selecting any one of a number of petals whose answer is 7 ($16 - 9 = ?; 6 + 1 = ?$).

Prescriptive teaching strategy 164:

Draw a ladder on the board with a number on each rung. On the bottom rung is a number and an arithmetic sign. The child has to add or subtract that number from the number appearing on each successive rung.

Prescriptive teaching strategy 165:

Design a hopscotch on the floor with masking tape and in each square mark an addition or subtraction problem. For every correct answer the child scores a point. At the conclusion of the activity the points for each child are tallied. The problems should be frequently changed to avoid memorization.

Multiplication and Division

Prescriptive teaching strategy 166:

The teacher prepares a set of twenty cards for common multiplication products. Each child is given a set of twenty problems or "question cards" (i.e., $4 \times 5 = ?; 5 \times 4 = ?$). She randomly selects one of her cards, presents it to the child and he must match it with an appropriate multiplication question. That is, in response to 20 the child may present any one of a number of cards such as $4 \times 5 = ?; 10 \times 2 = ?; 5 \times 4 = ?;$ or $20 \times 1 = ?$.

Prescriptive teaching strategy 167:

An exercise similar to strategy 166 may be developed for division facts.

Prescriptive teaching strategy 168:

Give each child a sheet of graph paper and a multiplication fact, such as $4 \times 3 = ?$. The student marks off on the graph paper four blocks down and three blocks across then totals the squares to derive the product.

Prescriptive teaching strategy 169:

Squares or rectangles are drawn on graph paper. Then the child is to determine how many groups are enclosed by the figures. For example, twenty-five graph blocks constitute five groups or sets of five. Next he writes an equation ($25 \div 5 = 5$) to represent his findings.

Prescriptive teaching strategy 170:

Draw a wagon wheel with a number on the hub and with different numbers on each of the sections divided by spokes. The pupil has to multiply the centre number by the number contained in each segment at the outside of the wheel.

Prescriptive teaching strategy 171:

Strategy 170 could also be used for division, with the number at the hub being the divisor.

Classification: the ability to group or categorize objects on the basis of common attributes.

Remedial Objective: to teach the child to recognize the common characteristics among objects.

Prescriptive teaching strategy 172:

Present the learner with plastic geometrical shapes of different colours and sizes. The child is asked to sort them by colour, size and shape.

Prescriptive teaching strategy 173:

Describe and illustrate the concepts of tall-short, large-small, up-down, first-last, more-less. Using paper circles of different diameters, have the children demonstrate the concepts by arranging the circles according to specific instructions such as from "largest to smallest in a left to right direction."

Prescriptive teaching strategy 174:
Ask the child to sort kitchen tableware into the appropriate sections of a plastic silverware tray.

Prescriptive teaching strategy 175:
Provide hoops constructed from plastic garden hose and ask the student to place objects inside that are of the same colour, shape or size.

Prescriptive teaching strategy 176:
Provide heavy and light objects to be sorted. Fill cans with different amounts of pebbles and cover them to conceal the amounts contained. The child sorts the containers into two groups—heavy and light. Next he arranges them from lightest to heaviest.

Prescriptive teaching strategy 177:
Call out a list consisting of fruits and vegetables and have the children determine in which category they belong. Categorization can be done with other objects.

Prescriptive teaching strategy 178:
The learner is given a collection of round, square and rectangular objects to be inserted into the appropriate shapes of a form board.

Prescriptive teaching strategy 179:
Display a group of objects with a common attribute and ask the pupil to identify the attribute, i.e., objects with windows, objects with roofs, objects with legs.

Prescriptive teaching strategy 180:
Give the student a deck of playing cards and have him sort them into suits. Next sort by colour—red, black and face cards.

Prescriptive teaching strategy 181:
Display a set with one extraneous object, i.e., pictures of a fork, knife, kitten and spoon. The child must discover which object does not belong and tell why it did not belong.

Prescriptive teaching strategy 182:
Instruct the learner to sort pictures of children's faces depicted in various activities into happy, surprised, angry and sad, i.e., a picture of a child licking a Hallowe'en sucker.

Prescriptive teaching strategy 183:

Prepare a scrapbook of "blue things," "tiny things," "moving things," "swimming things"; there are infinite variations.

Prescriptive teaching strategy 184:

Edibles which clearly fall into the categories of salt, sweet and bitter could be presented to the child to classify by taste, i.e., anchovies, corn syrup, grapefruit.

Prescriptive teaching strategy 185:

Present the child with about twenty words or pictures and have him pick out all the things that fit into a particular class, such as people, kitchen appliances and clothing.

Arithmetic Reasoning: the ability to apply the processes of addition, subtraction, multiplication and division.

Remedial Objective: to provide the child with learning opportunities which incorporate prior arithmetic fundamentals.

Prescriptive teaching strategy 186:

Use newspaper grocery advertisements in which prices are presented. Issue forty dollars in play money and the child pretends that he is purchasing a grocery order. He is asked to make various arithmetic computations related to grocery shopping such as sum of purchases (involving addition), change to be received (involving subtraction), the cost of several purchases of the same item (multiplication), and the cost per pound of selected produce (division).

Prescriptive teaching strategy 187:

An activity similar to strategy 186 could be developed around ordering a meal in a restaurant; menus, tips and payment of bill would be the foci.

Prescriptive teaching strategy 188:

Review what the children have learned about metric measurement and ask the pupil to measure the length and width of designated classroom objects.

Prescriptive teaching strategy 189:

Teaching of coinage equivalency might involve such activities as offering the student two sets of coins and asking him to decide which he would rather have after examining the composition of coins in each group. For example, which would you rather keep: two quarters, three dimes and a nickel or one quarter, two nickels, five pennies and a fifty-cent piece?

Prescriptive teaching strategy 190:

Present the 10 per cent sales tax in the context of personal purchases such as toys, games and hockey equipment. With older children the rudiments of income tax might be attempted using actual income tax forms and guidelines.

Prescriptive teaching strategy 191:

Prepare boxes numbered from 1 to 10 and cards on which are written equations such as ¼ of 12 = ? The pupil is given the cards and has to place each in the appropriate answer box.

Prescriptive teaching strategy 192:

The children may be exposed to elementary fractions as well as other aspects of practical measurement while using simple cooking recipes.

Prescriptive teaching strategy 193:

Egg cartons are very useful when presenting the concept of dozen, half dozen and one-third dozen.

Prescriptive teaching strategy 194:

Paper pie plates are a time-honoured and meaningful way of teaching simple fractions. Each child would be given a plate and asked to cut it into various fractional segments while closely following instruction and demonstration for the activity.

Prescriptive teaching strategy 195:

Fractions may be incorporated when teaching the concept of time, such as a half hour, a quarter hour and three-quarters of an hour. Draw a clock face on the floor using masking tape and divide the class into two teams. The teacher calls out a particular time such as half hour past 4 o'clock. Children from one of the teams indicate the time on the clock face by a child standing on the six and another standing on the four.

Prescriptive teaching strategy 196:

To familiarize children with the calendar, draw a big calendar for each month on the chalkboard. As the days pass, children mark in important events. In addition, it could be used to describe the weather, by writing in a weather symbol for each day. Children's birthdays, holidays and important class activities could be marked in appropriately.

Prescriptive teaching strategy 197:

Each student keeps a diary for in-class learning activities and recording time and events.

Prescriptive teaching strategy 198:

Teach the nursery rhyme: Thirty days hath September, April, June and November; all the rest hath thirty-one except February which stands alone.

Prescriptive teaching strategy 199:

Each day a different child writes the date and day of the week on the board while the rest of the students write it in their scribblers.

Prescriptive teaching strategy 200:

Children are paired for a simulated clock activity. Alternately, one child assumes the role of a clock positioning his hands so as to depict an hourly, half hourly or quarter hourly time. The second child must figure out the time being represented.

8/Reading Comprehension

Although much of what has been written about reading concerns the decoding segment of the process, reading comprehension is every bit as crucial if we choose to define reading as something more than sequential word calling.

According to Jenkinson (1973), reading traditionally has been defined as "the act of responding to printed symbols so that meaning is created." It is her view, however, that *obtaining meaning from* the page does not adequately describe what is going on in the reading process—it is too limited a definition. Rather, *bringing meaning to* the printed page more accurately indicates "the reciprocal process between the printed symbols and the mind of the reader." Within this framework, reading is viewed as a form of thinking, reasoning and problem-solving which involves a number of cognitive components such as analyzing, evaluating, discriminating and so on. Similarly, Karlin (1971) described reading as a "thinking and problem-solving process which involves not only the absorption of ideas but the creation of ideas." In brief, not only the construction of meaning but also the interpretation and evaluation of meaning must be included in any definition of the reading process.

Jenkinson's view represents the dichotomy which often is made between literal comprehension and comprehension at greater depth. Literal comprehension describes the most basic word, sentence and paragraph meaning; comprehension in depth incorporates the reader's interpretation, evaluation and reflections about the printed material.

Smith (1972) categorized reading in terms of depth of understanding, making reference to four levels: literal comprehension, interpretation, critical reading and creative reading. These levels are perceived as progressively more complex in terms of cognitive processing.

1. *Literal* comprehension is the most basic level involving the direct stated meaning of the author, that is, "reading the lines" of print;
2. *Interpretation* refers to gathering not only the literal surface meaning but also implied meaning, that is, "reading between the lines";

3. *Critical reading* refers to the application of a person's judgment and evaluation to the ideas presented, that is, "reading beyond the lines";
4. *Creative reading* involves the ability to generate ideas and insights from exposure to the material. It is at the apex of reading comprehension skill development.

Bond and Tinker (1967) presented a developmental sequence in reading comprehension extending from single word meaning to the comprehension of larger units. This framework parallels and complements the developmental trend from literal to higher levels of comprehension presented earlier. The functionally interrelated sequence is presented in summary:

1. *Word meanings:* the acquisition of word meaning is a fundamental prerequisite to all comprehension in reading. Without satisfactory word meanings, comprehension of either spoken or printed language is impossible.
2. *Thought units:* the inability to group material into thought units— which is the problem with children who read one word at a time or groups of words inappropriately—is an obstacle to effective sentence comprehension.
3. *Sentence comprehension:* in addition to understanding the meanings of separate words and thought units, there must be the ability to understand the relationship between those used in a sentence. If the child cannot sense the relationship between elements within a sentence and assign each its proper relative importance, the result is severe difficulties in comprehension.
4. *Paragraph comprehension:* satisfactory comprehension of the material in a paragraph is possible only when the reader understands the relation between the sentences which make up the paragraph.
5. *Comprehending larger units:* to grasp the organization of an expository article or a story, the reader must understand the relation between the theme or purpose presented in the introductory paragraphs and the role of the succeeding supporting paragraphs.

Niles (1963) presents three abilities which differentiate between the reader who comprehends well and the one who does not:

1. The power to find and understand thought relationships: in single sentences, in paragraphs and in selections of varying lengths;
2. The ability to set specific purposes in reading;
3. The ability to make full use of previous learning in attacking new material.

According to Niles, the acquisition of these skills can be facilitated to some extent by the teacher choosing the correct questions to pose to her students. The teacher must probe beyond a mere check for accuracy and superficial meaning. She must coax out the student's ability to focus upon meaningful associations, to assimilate and to interpret. When this takes place, reading becomes more of a learning experience. Along the same line of thought Spache and Spache (1973) cite two influences upon the reader's retention:

1. His purpose in reading (what he intends to retain);
2. The instructions he is given before reading. The teacher's instructions may lead the student to find precise answers to specific questions in some cases; to secure a broader, more general comprehension in other cases.

Developmentally it is true that the young reader appropriates more time to the decoding process than to comprehension. As the child becomes older this relationship reverses and the mechanics of decoding fade into the background. This does not mean that they cannot be summoned on occasion when a problematic new word is encountered. Generally speaking, with age and experience, comprehension at progressively more advanced levels comes to the foreground of the reading experience.

There are a number of factors which can adversely influence the development of comprehension skills. It goes almost without saying that poor attention, experiential deficits, and general language retardation undermine the decoding segment of the reading process as well as comprehension. Similarly, a perceptual problem in the auditory and/or visual modality, as described earlier, can destroy reading comprehension inasmuch as it destroys the decoding process itself. Word, sentence and paragraph meaning even at the literal level of comprehension are subverted proportional to the severity of a perceptual handicap.

For a number of children who have comprehension problems, the difficulty stems from the mechanics of decoding print. Heilman (1961) stated that reading rate relates to comprehension in various ways. If a child has inadequate word-attack skills which prevent pronunciation of the words he encounters, he will ponder over individual words and become a word-by-word reader. Such a child will lose meaning as he concentrates on the individual words rather than on the thought unit. Also, if the child attempts to hurry, reading comprehension deteriorates as a function of the increased pressure to perform quickly. As pointed out by Spache and Spache (1973) rapid reading contributes to better understanding "only when the material is easy or familiar, and the rate of reading approximates the reader's speed for associating ideas."

A comprehensive list of disabilities in the area of reading comprehension is presented by Farrald (1971). When considering the list it is easy to see how hopelessly lost a child would feel in terms of the total school curriculum if he had a reading comprehension problem. Such a problem would be pervasive to the entire learning process, cutting through various content areas—sciences, history, literature, mathematics and so on.

Inadequate meaning vocabulary.
Inability to grasp details.
Inability to grasp thought units.
Inability to comprehend the main idea.
Inability to classify and list facts in a sensible manner.
Inability to establish a sequence.
Inability to follow a series of related directions.
Inability to sense relationships.
Inability to distinguish between the major ideas and the related facts.
Evaluation: inability to differentiate between fact and fancy.
Inability to judge reasonableness and relevancy of ideas presented.
Inability to sense implied meanings.
Inability to establish cause and effect relationships.
Inability to judge the authenticity or validity of materials and presentation.
Interpretation: lack of understanding the significance of a selection beyond the statements of the author.
Inability to make comparisons.
Inability to draw an inference or conclusion not expressly stated.
Inability to predict outcome.
Reluctance in forming one's own opinion.
Inability to infer time and measure relationships.
Appreciation: inability to understand the feeling and tone developed by the authors.
Inability to sense the plot, humour and author's feelings.
Inability to form sensory impressions.
Lack of understanding of personal qualities of the characters.
(Reading Comprehension Disabilities Checklist, Farrald, 1971)

Meaning vocabularies vary greatly from child to child. That is, the child who enters school from a disadvantaged home does not have as large a meaning vocabulary as the child whose background is filled with travel and other enriching experiences. And, although it would be ideal if each child could build an elaborate meaning vocabulary through experience, the school curriculum does not allow sufficient time to provide such experiences as would be necessary to illustrate the meaning of *all* new words. Consequently, in order to help improve reading comprehension, the teacher must be aware of various facilitating strategies. The students must be taught to use their own and other strategies to ascertain word meaning.

Although it is agreed that reading comprehension encompasses literal, interpretive, critical and creative levels, the remainder of our discussion will centre upon literal meaning, the most basic level of comprehension. As expressed by Karlin (1971), "there is no doubt that the acquisition of literal meaning is fundamental and a precursor to other kinds of reading performances."

Word Meaning

Word meaning is absolutely essential to literal comprehension and is basic to higher levels of comprehension. Thus it is imperative that the reading teacher be familiar with methods used to help derive word meaning—contextual clues, morpheme clues, word form clues, dictionary skills and so on.

Context clues. Since word meaning characterizes the most basic level of reading comprehension, it is extremely important that the child learn to use aids such as context clues to decode new words. The ability to anticipate word meaning from the surrounding words can be taught through direct instruction in most cases. This is not to say that every child will be equally adept at this skill or that all new words can be given a clear-cut meaning from context. It is reasonable, however, to think that the meaning of the printed word *foot* might be facilitated by context clues such as those provided in the sentence, "She put the green and yellow sock on her foot."

In a related fashion, picture clues can provide the child with some idea of word meaning. In a well-illustrated book a sailing picture might provide expectancy clues as the child encounters the new word *sailor* or *lighthouse* in his reading.

In some cases the author defines a word within the written text providing a direct context clue. According to Karlin (1971) this may be done by an actual definition, a synonym, or illustration.

The captain *testified*, or gave evidence, during the trial.

The Inuit use a *kayak*, which is a light, sealskin boat, the top of which is covered over except for a hole where the hunter sits.

A *stoneboat* is a low sled, sometimes having shaped log-runners, used for removing stones from fields and for other heavy hauling.

Kennedy (1971) lists several abilities that are related to the use of context. For effective use of context clues the student should be able to:
1. Make a close guess at the pronunciation of a word from its use in a sentence;
2. Suggest a word from a written or oral definition;
3. Find synonyms to replace meaningful words in a sentence;
4. Arrange words into meaningful sentences;
5. Arrange sentence parts into an understandable whole.

Morphemic clues: A morpheme is the smallest unit of language that carries meaning. The word *cover* is a single morpheme whereas *uncover* contains two morphemes—*cover,* and the prefix *un* which means "not." Prefixes, suffixes, root words, and the parts of compound words are meaning units or morphemes. During the course of teaching, children can be made aware of morphemes as they are encountered, thus providing an aid when new words are presented. A knowledge of *re* in the word *return* would help in discovering the meaning of recall, react, replace, redistribute, and so on.

Structural analysis, a well-established form of word attack, studies the morphemes and word parts which have been blended to form whole words. Prefixes, suffixes, syllabication, compound words, base or root words, and contractions are used in this form of analysis.

Word form clues: These clues are utilized to help recognize a word by its overall shape, configuration or form. When a person is an efficient reader he needs only to see the first few letters of a word or its general form in order to recognize it.

Kennedy (1971) states that a number of abilities are necessary if a student is to benefit from word form or configuration clues. He should be able to:

1. See the differences between such letters as *b, d, q, p;*
2. Recognize by sight most words that have been taught;
3. Remember words easily that have been taught as sight words;
4. Recognize the difference between such words as *through* and *thorough, very* and *every,* and *was* and *saw;*
5. Copy words accurately from flashed exercises.

Sometimes the unique configuration of a word can be illustrated by outlining it. This type of clue should be considered as supplementary, used in combination with other context clues. In a strict sense, word form clues relate to word recognition rather than word meaning. Nevertheless, they may be of value to the child who finds it necessary to approach reading in terms of a sight word vocabulary.

Multiple meaning and dictionary skills: Some words change their meaning with context. If a child is not aware of this he will have difficulty when a familiar word is presented in a unique context. Obviously, the teacher cannot be expected to cover the multiplicity of words which have various meanings in any systematic fashion. According to Karlin (1971) the teacher might best be advised "to establish attitudes that cause children to react to words in a thoughtful and flexible way."

On some occasions specific opportunities to build new word meanings grow out of discussions with the students or from language experiences. Possibly the teacher and students might select a word such as *catch* and develop sentences to illustrate various meanings.

He did not think that he would *catch* a cold so late in April.
The men in the boat were disappointed with their meager *catch*.
Catch the ball, Fred.
The *catch* on the door was rusted beyond repair.

It goes almost without saying that dictionary skills are important for approaching some new words. In the upper elementary grades the use of guide words should be given emphasis so that the child can easily locate the word he is seeking. These skills can be taught through direct instruction, possibly during the spelling or reading period.

Sentence Meaning

The ability to relate words meaningfully into larger units—sentences, paragraphs, stories—is the natural extension of literal comprehension beyond basic word meaning. According to Karlin (1971), sentence structure is simple and straightforward during the initial stages of reading, but as reading materials become more advanced, sentences become more complex, filled with phrases and modifiers. Explanation of basic subject-predicate sentence structure as two parts—one which tells *who* or *what*, another which provides information about who or what—sometimes helps the reader find his way through a long cumbersome sentence. Also, rewriting long complex sentences in the form of several shorter, simple sentences can help the child reread the original.

Karlin has pointed out that a basic knowledge of the function of common punctuation marks can be very beneficial in understanding sentence meaning. In some cases punctuation changes the entire meaning of a sentence.

Woman without her man is a savage.
Woman, without her man is a savage.
or
The sheriff has left town!
The sheriff has left town.
The sheriff has left town?

Another problem related to sentence meaning is created by pronouns separated by phrases, clauses and modifiers from their referents. Young readers will often have difficulty deciding what *it*, *him* or *they* refer to in a sentence which has a number of possible referents for a pronoun.

The hunters and their dogs, after abandoning the sled which had become encased in ice, moved further and further from *it* and the supplies *they* so desperately needed.

After having properly matched pronouns with referents, the meaning of the sentence becomes apparent. Karlin (1971) suggests that by locating the word a pronoun stands for in the sentence, and substituting it in place of the pronoun, the child can check his matching.

Longer Units

To understand longer units (paragraphs, essays, stories) the reader must be able to relate the several single words and sentences to form a larger meaning unit. Often this is facilitated by the writer's style. According to Harris (1970) *good writing* can be equated with *organized writing* in that the author begins with a clear conception of what he wants to say and "thinks out the order, sequence, relative importance and interrelatedness of the specific ideas he intends to convey." The better the child discerns the author's plan or pattern the greater will be his understanding.

When teaching a child to follow the organizational pattern of longer passages of printed material, the teacher must encourage the child to consider the various possible ways in which the material may be structured. Cause and effect, comparison and contrast, time sequence, topic, and enumeration are common patterns in paragraph organization. As noted by Bond and Tinker (1967) the reader must perceive the relationship between the theme or purpose set out in the introductory paragraphs and the part played by succeeding supporting paragraphs when attempting to understand larger units.

As reading comprehension advances beyond the literal level to inferential and critical levels, the child must move beyond the printed line to draw conclusions, predict outcomes, make inferences, see relationships, question presented facts, separate fact from opinion, and perform a host of other skills related to reading comprehension. Although some of the strategies which follow are aimed at the development of comprehension skills above the literal level, the teacher is directed toward the sources cited in this chapter, such as Karlin (1971), for a more comprehensive review of both theory and practical suggestions related to advanced levels of comprehension.

Suggested Strategies

Reading Comprehension: the ability to understand words in print at various levels of meaning—literal, interpretive, critical and creative levels.

Remedial Objective: To help pupils first achieve literal comprehension of printed words, eventually leading to analyzing and interpreting the author's ideas.

Prescriptive teaching strategy 201:

Give children a list of semantically related words in which one word does not belong, for example, large, little, small, tiny. Ask the child to find the word which does not belong and explain why it does not fit the category.

Prescriptive teaching strategy 202:

Prepare riddles and ask the children to select from possible answers. The child considers each and tells why it is or is not a suitable answer.

Prescriptive teaching strategy 203:

Write two columns of words with the words in column II being opposite in meaning to the words in column I. The positioning of words in column II is such that the words are not aligned with their opposites. Children draw lines to connect each word with its opposite.

Prescriptive teaching strategy 204:

After the students have completed an exciting activity, the teacher writes an account of it, using students' suggestions. After it is written, several key words are omitted. These are written on file cards (one word per card) and are intermixed with other word cards. The child is given all the file cards and he has to correctly place the missing words in the teacher's account of the activity.

Prescriptive teaching strategy 205:

In column I, write a definition which is suited to the vocabulary level of the class. In column II, write the word which has been defined. The words in the second column must not align with their definitions. For example: You can sew with this—needle. A time limit may be set for completing the task.

Prescriptive teaching strategy 206:

Ask a child to describe another student in the class. The other children in the class have to try to discover who is being described. It is very important for the describer to avoid directly looking at the person he is describing because this gives the children an immediate clue as to the identity of the person being described.

Prescriptive teaching strategy 207:

Select words which are not within the reading vocabulary of the class and write them in sentences. The children must find the correct meaning from context cues.

Prescriptive teaching strategy 208:

Explain prefixes, suffixes and root words to the class. Next, present a list of words which the children must carefully analyze. Skills from these exercises should provide guides to meaning of new words.

Prescriptive teaching strategy 209:

Present sentences in which the context is coupled with initial phonic elements as aids to word recognition, e.g., "He will paint the fender on the b_____ (boat, carriage, bicycle, balloon)."

Prescriptive teaching strategy 210:

Make a list of sentences each having one word missing. The children are instructed to provide a suitable word to complete the sentence.

Prescriptive teaching strategy 211:

Cut out short comic strips with dialogue from the newspaper; jumble the story. The child is given the pieces and has to assemble them in the proper sequence.

Prescriptive teaching strategy 212:

Each child is given a paragraph to read and after he has read it, he may illustrate on a piece of paper his ideas by using water paints or crayons. This provides a check of the pupil's interpretation of content.

Prescriptive teaching strategy 213:

Direct the children to read a tale which has the concluding sentence (or paragraph) omitted. They must review the events and decide what might be a suitable ending for the story.

Prescriptive teaching strategy 214:

Give each child a different paragraph to read followed by three suggested titles. Instruct the child to read the paragraph silently and choose the appropriate title. Next, the paragraph is read aloud and each student has to discuss reasons for his choice.

Prescriptive teaching strategy 215:

Construct a five sentence paragraph putting the sentences in random order. The purpose of the activity is for the child to recognize that sentences must be placed in a logical sequence if they are to form a paragraph. The sentences may be written on strips of cardboard and the child asked to arrange them appropriately.

Prescriptive teaching strategy 216:

Present two statements concerning nature studies, one of which is fact and one of which is personal opinion. Have the children decide which is fact and which is opinion. Ask them to decide whether a statement of fact or opinion is the most accurate.

Prescriptive teaching strategy 217:

Give the children a story to read and ask them to write their interpretation. This is an activity where there can be lively and stimulating discussion. If the students are taught to criticize constructively and offer suggestions, it can be a valuable social learning experience.

Prescriptive teaching strategy 218:

Fully describe a scene with two main characters; then, have the students write their interpretation of what might happen, making inferences from the descriptions which have been given.

Prescriptive teaching strategy 219:

Read an interesting story aloud and stop occasionally to ask the children to discuss what the next word or phrase might be.

Prescriptive teaching strategy 220:

Read a story to the children and then instruct them to retell it in their own words.

Prescriptive teaching strategy 221:

Read a story and prepare a list of true and false statements based upon it. The children must state whether each sentence is true or false.

Prescriptive teaching strategy 222:

Choose from two or three paragraphs the one which would provide the best conclusion to a story which has been presented.

Prescriptive teaching strategy 223:

A complete story is read to the students who must select the most logical and the most illogical ending from five ending choices written on the chalkboard.

Prescriptive teaching strategy 224:

Present sentences in which there are figures of speech such as similes and metaphors. Instruct the children to locate these and tell what they mean, i.e., "A fish is like a skate" or some other appropriate figure of speech.

References

Ayres, A. J. "Tactile functions: Their relation to hyperactive and perceptual-motor behavior." *American Journal of Occupational Therapy,* 1964, *18,* 6-11.

Baker, G. P., and Raskin, L. M. "Sensory integration in the learning disabled." *Journal of Learning Disabilities,* 1973, *6,* 645-649.

Barraga, N. *Visual handicaps and learning.* Belmont, Calif.: Wadsworth, 1976.

Barrett, T. C. "Visual discrimination tasks as predictors of first-grade reading achievement." *Reading Teacher,* 1965, *18,* 276-282.

Bauer, B. A. "Tactile-sensitive behavior in hyperactive and non-hyperactive children." *American Journal of Occupational Therapy,* 1977, *31,* 447-453.

Bereiter, C. *Arithmetic and mathematics.* San Rafael, Calif.: Dimensions Publishing, 1968.

Bishop, V. E. *Teaching the visually limited child.* Springfield, Ill.: Thomas, 1971.

Blau, H., and Blau, H. "A theory of learning to read by 'Modality Blocking'." In J. Arena (Ed.), *Successful programming: Many points of view.* Pittsburgh: Association for Children with Learning Disabilities, 1969.

Bond, G. L., and Tinker, M. A. *Reading difficulties: Their diagnosis and correction.* New York: Appleton-Century-Crofts, 1967.

Bortner, M. *Evaluation and education of children with brain damage.* Springfield, Ill.: Thomas, 1968.

Buckhout, R. Cited in National Report. *Intellect,* 1975, *103,* 423-424.

Carhart, R. "Auditory training." In H. Davis and S. R. Silverman (Eds.), *Hearing and deafness* (2nd ed.). New York: Holt, Rinehart, 1960.

Carter, H., and McGinnis, D. J. *Diagnosis and treatment of the disabled reader.* London: Collier-MacMillan, 1970.

Casler, L. "The effects of extra tactile stimulation on a group of institutionalized infants." *Genetic Psychology Monographs,* 1965, *71,* 137-175.

Chalfant, J. C., and Flathouse, V. E. "Auditory and visual learning." In H. R. Mykelbust (Ed.), *Progress in learning disabilities* (Vol. 1). New York: Grune & Stratton, 1971.

Chalfant, J. C., and Scheffelin, M. A. *Central processing dysfunctions in children: A review of research.* Washington, D.C.: U.S. Government Printing Office, 1969.

Chaney, C. M., and Kephart, N. C. *Motoric Aids to perceptual training.* Columbus, Ohio: C. E. Merrill, 1968.

Cohn, R. Developmental dyscalculia. *Pediatrics Clinics of America,* 1968, *15,* 651-668. (a)

————. *Developmental disorders of motility and language.* Philadelphia: Saunders, 1968. (b)

Cruickshank, W. M., Bentzen, F. A., Ratzeburg, F. H., and Tannhauser, M. T. *A Teaching Method for Brain-Injured and Hyperactive Children.* Syracuse, N.Y.: Syracuse University Press, 1961.

Cruickshank, W., and Johnson, O. *Educating exceptional children and youth.* Englewood Cliffs, N.J.: Prentice-Hall, 1975.

Dantzig, T. *Number—the language of science.* New York: Macmillan, 1939.

Davis, H. "Audiometry: Pure tone and simple speech tests." In H. Davis and S. R. Silverman (Eds.), *Hearing and deafness* (3rd ed.). New York: Holt, Rinehart, 1970.

Dechant, E. *Diagnosis and remediation of reading disability.* West Nyack, N.Y.: Parker, 1968.

Faas, L. A. *Learning disabilities: A competency based approach.* Boston: Houghton Mifflin, 1976.

Farrald, R. R. *A remediation handbook for children with reading disabilities.* Sioux Falls, South Dakota: Adapt Press, 1971.

Farrald, R. R., and Schamber, R. G. *A mainstream approach to identification, assessment and amelioration of learning disabilities.* Sioux Falls, South Dakota: Adapt Press, 1973.

Fernald, G. M. *Remedial techniques in basic school subjects.* New York: McGraw-Hill, 1943.

Fisher, S. "Body awareness and selective memory for body versus non-body references." *Journal of Personality,* 1964, *33,* 536-552.

Friedus, E. "The needs of teachers for special information on number concepts." In W. Cruickshank (Ed.), *The teacher of brain-injured children.* Syracuse, N.Y.: Syracuse University Press, 1966.

Gearheart, B. R. *Teaching the learning disabled.* Saint Louis: Mosby, 1973.

———. *Learning disabilities: Educational strategies* (2nd ed.). Saint Louis: Mosby, 1973.

Gesell, A., and Amatruda, C. *Developmental diagnosis.* New York: P. B. Hoeber, 1947.

Gibson, J. J. *The senses considered as perceptual systems.* Boston: Houghton Mifflin, 1966.

Gillingham, A., and Stillman, B. W. *Remedial training for children with specific disability in reading, spelling, and penmanship* (7th ed.). Cambridge, Mass.: Educators Publishing Service, 1968.

Hallahan, D. P., and Kauffman, J. M. *Introduction to learning disabilities: The cycle behavioral approach.* Englewood Cliffs, N.J.: Prentice-Hall, 1976.

Hammill, D. D., and Bartel, N. R. *Teaching children with learning and behavior problems.* Boston: Allyn & Bacon, 1975.

Harris, A. J. *How to increase reading ability* (5th ed.). New York: David McKay, 1970.

Heilman, A. W. *Principles and practices of teaching reading.* Columbus, Ohio: C. E. Merrill, 1961.

Hirsh, I. J. Auditory training. In H. Davis and S. R. Silverman (Eds.), *Hearing and deafness* (3rd ed.). New York: Holt, Rinehart, 1970.

Jenkinson, M. D. "Ways of teaching." In R. C. Staiger (Ed.), *The teacher of reading.* Lexington, Mass.: Ginn, 1973.

Johnson, D. J. , and Myklebust, H. R. *Learning disabilities: Educational principles and practices.* New York: Grune & Stratton, 1967.

Jones, M. G. "Perception, personality and movement (M.Ed. dissertation, University of Leicester, England, 1970). *Index to Theses,* 1969-70, *20,* No. 1481.

Kaliski, L. "Arithmetic and the brain-injured child." *Arithmetic Teacher,* 1962, *9,* 245-251.

Karlin, R. *Teaching elementary reading: Principles and strategies.* New York: Harcourt, Brace, Jovanovich, 1971.

Kennedy, E. C. *Classroom approaches to remedial reading.* Ithaca, Ill.: Peacock Publishers, 1971.

Kosc, L. "Developmental dyscalculia." *Journal of Learning Disabilities,* 1974, *7,* 164-176.

Lerner, J. W. *Children with learning disabilities.* Boston: Houghton Mifflin, 1976.

Levy, R. B. *I can only touch you now.* Englewood Cliffs, N.J.: Prentice-Hall, 1973.

McKibbin, E. H. "The effect of additional tactile stimulation in a perceptual-motor program for school children." *The American Journal of Occupational Therapy,* 1973, *27,* 191-197.

Miller, W. H. *Diagnosis and correction of reading difficulties in secondary school students.* New York: Center for Applied Research in Education, 1973.

Money, J. (Ed.). *Reading disability: Progress and research needs in dyslexia.* Baltimore: J. Hopkins, 1962.

Montagu, A. *Prenatal influences.* Springfield, Ill. Thomas, 1962.

Montessori, M. *The Montessori Method.* New York: F. A. Stokes, 1912.

—————. *Dr. Montessori's Own Handbook.* New York: F. A. Stokes, 1914.

Morris, P. R., and Whiting, H. T. A. *Motor impairment and compensatory education.* London: Bell, 1971.

Murch, G. M. *Visual and auditory perception.* Indianapolis: Bobbs-Merrill, 1973.

National Society for the Prevention of Blindness. *Teaching about vision.* New York: Author, 1972.

Niles, O. S. Comprehension skills. *Reading Teacher,* 1963, *17,* 2-7.

Otto, H. A. "Sensory awakening through smell, touch, and taste." In H. A. Otto and J. Mann (Eds.), *Ways of growth: Approaches to expanding human awareness.* New York: Viking Press, 1968.

Pfeiffer, J. W., and Jones, J. E. *A handbook of structured experiences for human relations training* (Vol. 2). Iowa City, Iowa: University Associates Press, 1970.

Piaget, J. "How children form mathematical concepts." *Scientific American,* 1953, *189* (5), 74-79.

Raskin, L. M., and Baker, G. P. "Tactual and visual integration in the learning process: Research and implications." *Journal of Learning Disabilities,* 1975, *8,* 108-112.

Ross, A. O. *Psychological aspects of learning disabilities & reading disorders.* New York: McGraw-Hill, 1976.

Sanders, D. A. *Aural Rehabilitation.* Englewood Cliffs, N.J.: Prentice-Hall, 1971.

Segel, R. C. "Improving perception through the haptic process." *Academic Therapy,* 1974, *9,* 420-424.

Shiffrin, R. M., and Atkinson, R. C. "Storage and retrieval processes in long-term memory." *Psychological Review,* 1969, *76,* 179-193.

Silver, A. A., and Hagin, R. "Specific reading disability: Dilineation of the syndrome and relationship to cerebral dominance." *Comprehensive Psychiatry,* 1960, *1,* 126-134.

Smith, N. B. "The many faces of reading comprehension." In L. Harris and C. Smith (Eds.), *Individualizing reading instruction: A reader.* New York: Holt, Rinehart, 1972.

Solomon, P. *Sensory deprivation.* Cambridge: Harvard University Press, 1965.

Spache, G. D., and Spache, E. B. *Reading in the elementary school.* Boston: Allyn & Bacon, 1973.

Squires, D. Specific learning disabilities related to mathematics. Unpublished manuscript, Memorial University, 1976.

Stevens, G. *Movement activities for children with learning disabilities.* Toronto: Ontario Association for Children with Learning Disabilities, 1971.

Stone, R. E. "Relation between the perception and reproduction of body postures." *Research Quarterly,* 1968, *39,* 721-727.

Thurlow, W. R. "Audition." In J. W. Kling and L. A. Riggs (Eds.), *Experimental Psychology.* New York: Holt, Rinehart, 1971.

Verdelin, J. *The mathematical ability.* Lund-Copenhagen: CWK Cleerup, 1958.

Wallace, G., and McLoughlin, J. A. *Learning disabilities: Concepts and characteristics.* Columbus, Ohio: C. E. Merrill, 1975.

Wepman, J. M. "The modality concept—including a statement of the perceptual and conceptual levels of learning." In *Perception and reading.* Conference Proceedings of the International Reading Association, 1968, *8,* 1-6.

West, C. J., and Foster, S. F. *The psychology of human learning and instruction in education.* Belmont, Calif.: Wadsworth, 1976.

White, M., Lefroy, R., and Weston, D. *Treating reading disabilities.* San Rafael, Calif.: Academic Therapy, 1975.

Zentall, S. S. "Optimal stimulation as theoretical basis of hyperactivity." *American Journal of Orthopsychiatry,* 1975, *45,* 549-563.

Zentall, S. S. "Environmental stimulation model." *Exceptional Children, 43,* 1977, 502-510.